To Debbie
Thanks for
being th...
love Judith
x.

Proven Strategies for Success

People often refer to the 4 P's of Marketing as;

Price, Product, Place and Promotion,

but in this fascinating book these 4 P's have a new twist;

People, Passion, Pioneering and…Purple!

Hold on to your hair… this will be quite a journey!

by Judith Wright

WRIGHT ANGLE MARKETING

www.wrightanglemarketing.com

Proven Strategies for Success

Published by Judith Wright

WRIGHT
ANGLE
MARKETING

Wright Angle Marketing
Unit 70 Bowers Mill, Branch Road, Barkisland, West Yorkshire HX4 0AD
www.wrightanglemarketing.com

A catalogue record for this book is available
from the British Library.

ISBN 978-0-9931630-0-5

Printed and distributed by IngramSpark
Ingram DV LLC Attn:General Counsel
14 Ingram Boulevard, La Vergne, TN 37086. Fax: 615-213-5080

	Foreword	*iv*
	Introduction	*1*
Chapter One	People	*11*
Chapter Two	Passion	*53*
Chapter Three	Pioneering	*85*
Chapter Four	Purple!	*133*

Contents

Foreword

If I had to describe myself, I would say I am somebody who loves life. In fact, people have always been at the heart of everything I have ever done. At fourteen, I was working in a newsagents at weekends and in school holidays. In fact, at times, I managed the shop on my own when staff were away - I'm not sure that would be allowed anymore! On weekdays I looked after two children straight after school.

When I was nineteen, I started my own hairdressing business. At the time I thought it was the scariest thing ever. The business really took off and we got busier each year. I was a national award winning hairdresser, but I still maintain that it was my ability to connect with people that brought the customers in by the dozen. I then bought a second shop and the guy we bought it off told us he was coming out of hairdressing. In reality he opened another shop within the locality and took a lot of his customers with him. This resulted in an uphill struggle to build the business.

I was experiencing a lot of health challenges with my back and in the end I was told by the medics that unless I changed my job it wouldn't improve.

So I decided to do a teaching qualification so I could pass on my hairdressing skills within a teaching environment. We sold two shops, a house and another property we rented out all on the same weekend. So I suddenly found myself in the very new position of being unemployed, well, apart from doing some part time teaching hours at two colleges.

Within four months I had secured a full time teaching post. The job had a responsibility for the marketing of the hair and beauty section. I discovered I loved marketing and once again decided to have a change in career. I decided to go and get my marketing qualifications, and move into the world of marketing. Eventually I applied for and got a job as a Marketing Officer in a Further Education college. I progressed to Marketing Manager and eventually became an Assistant Director of the college. This experience lasted for quite a few years and I loved the job.

Over time the environment I was working in changed and I didn't feel it was the right place for me anymore. At the same time I was suffering with terrible back problems and I was off work for three months.

I am not sure how quickly I should have recovered but the hospital intervention, which involved one spine, numerous bent needles and multiple shots of cortisone, didn't seem to help much.

When the hospital took to ringing me at home to see how I was, and saying things like, "Well it isn't what we would normally have used, but it should have been OK." I began to get seriously worried. Looking back, I realise that every time I wasn't happy with the environment I was in, my back troubles flared up. I now absolutely believe in the link between what's going on in our mind and the physical effect it has on our body, but I guess that's a story for another day.

I decided that I didn't want to be at the college anymore as I didn't feel it was a very healthy environment for me. So I made what felt like a huge decision to hand in my notice. I had no idea what I was going to do, but I just knew I didn't want to be where I was anymore. I rang my husband from work one morning and said, "You know that I keep talking about leaving work? Well I am going to do it." He said, "Oh, well we will talk about it tonight." I said, "No, I am handing it in at 7.30am when my boss arrives." Which I did. As you can imagine, we had a very interesting conversation in my house later that day.

At that point I had no idea what I wanted to do but, within a day, I had decided I was going to work for myself, as I loved Marketing. Thirteen years on and I am still loving my job as MD of Wright Angle Marketing Ltd.

Over the last thirteen years I have worked with and for some amazing personalities and businesses. These have ranged from start-up businesses, to national and international companies. The turnover of those companies has also been wide ranging, from lifestyle businesses to multi million pound concerns. The factors that are constant in the successful businesses I have worked with is that there is always passion and a thirst to learn and develop. I believe these two factors go hand in hand with business success.

Life hasn't always been a bed of roses, but I am grateful for all the experiences life has given me because, without them, I would not be who I am today. Even the guy who I felt had shafted me in business, when I finally met up with him again years later I shook his hand and thanked him, because without that experience, my life would have taken a completely different course and I would not be here today sharing this book with you.

Judith Wright 

Thank you

I would like to take this opportunity to say a huge thank you to everyone whose lives have touched mine be it briefly, or for a longer period of time, be it in the present or in the past.

I owe you all a huge debt of gratitude because each and every one of you has played a part in making me the person I am today, and for that I will be eternally grateful.

Introduction

Launching a business is exciting. It's also a little bit scary! After all, you probably have a lot of hopes and dreams for your business but you can't help but be aware of the fact that many businesses don't make it out of their first year. In fact, 50% of businesses fail within the first year, and 95% of them fail within five years.

What gives the 5% of businesses that do survive the power to do so? Did they start out with more capital than the other 95%? Did they stay out of debt? Did they just come up with a better product than everyone else? Perhaps those business owners had more charisma or better connections.

Actually, this lucky 5% does *not* necessarily have more money or a better product than all of the businesses that fail. Nor do they necessarily have more privileged owners.

Often the products sold by these businesses are quite ordinary. In fact, the people behind these successful products and services are often equally ordinary!

The success stories just have a very different mindset about the force that drives their business forward and allows them to make money. They understand that force and they understand that they must make it a high priority. That force is **marketing**!

Many business owners are actually rather uncomfortable with the prospect of marketing. As a result, these business owners decide that marketing is secondary to everything they're trying to do. In reality, if you're in any business at all you are, to some degree, in the marketing business. Businesses exist to sell products and services. Sales don't happen without leads. You need a steady stream of interested individuals to talk to about your products and services. Leads don't happen without marketing because if you don't market your business nobody knows that your fantastic new products or services exist in the first place. Customers will go to the mediocre competitor they know about over the invisible superstar, and who could blame them, they didn't know about you.

Most people who go into business do so because they have a particular skill or passion. We *love* passion at Wright Angle Marketing (WAM), because we're passionate too. We're passionate about the success of each and every one of our clients.

Proven Strategies for Success

We just happen to know that **passion can't do the job on its own—and neither can skill**. You could be the very best at what you do and still fail in your business because nobody knows about it. Your offering could be the one thing that millions upon millions of consumers have been waiting for—and nobody will buy it if you don't get your marketing right, preferably right at the very beginning, at the starting gate, so that you survive that first year.

I think many people are so uncomfortable with marketing because we're all taught not to brag as children, and marketing feels a little bit like bragging. Nobody wants to be impolite, after all. We've all seen pushy, hyped-up adverts that make wild promises, and sometimes we've even bought products or services in response to those ads. Then, those products and services did not live up to the promises that were made. You felt duped and your money was gone.
If these experiences have left a bad taste in your mouth you're not alone. Most people would rather do just about *anything* than 'be sold' something they don't want or need.

Fortunately, there are plenty of ways to market your business that are neither rude nor pushy. You can be completely honest about who you are, what your business does, and how it helps others.

At WAM, we teach people to be 100% truthful when they communicate with customers and potential customers. Indeed, we're going to teach you how to be a little bit more insightful about your business because if you don't understand your business you could end up fibbing about it without even meaning to!

In fact, when you market the 'WAM way' you'll be doing your customers a favour because you'll be building bridges between their problems and the solutions to those problems. You're going to be very specific about the people you reach out to. When you finally speak to those people, you will do so knowing that you are giving them the information they need.

That's good news because marketing is the *only* way to secure new customers for your business. If you can't secure new customers you're going to go out of business—it's that simple. Spontaneous word of mouth is nice, but it's a little bit like winning the lottery. You can't *force* it to happen. You can, however, increase your opportunities. As more people learn about your business you get more 'tickets' because this increases the cross section of people who might become 'brand ambassadors' on your behalf. You can control how well you communicate with your target audience and how often you do so.

Proven Strategies for Success

You can control where you go to communicate with your target audience. You can give yourself and your business the best chance to succeed by understanding what it means to market your business and embracing the need to do it.

Now, we're not going to write you an instruction manual on every marketing method that's available. Those methods—called channels—are the tactical part of marketing: the short-term, boots-on-the-ground techniques that you can use to get your message across. It's quite useful to study these channels but that's not what we're about here. There are other books that will tell you exactly how to succeed on social media, how to take advantage of search engine optimisation, where and how to place an advertorial and when a billboard might be appropriate. We will talk a little bit about those channels, but not in any technical sense.

Instead, we're inviting you to put on your MO hat for the very first time (that is, your 'Marketing Officer' hat) and to learn all about marketing *strategy.* When you understand the strategy behind small business marketing, you can make solid decisions about the future of your company. Focusing on strategy will keep you from dumping money into endless banner ads, just because banner ads seem good to you.

It will keep you from spending all of your time trying to run a Facebook campaign when your time or energy might be better served working on or in some other part of your business. Strategy helps you decide *what* should be done, *when* it should be done, *why* it should be done, and *who* should to it. You're also going to learn about the realities that should drive your strategies.

Many marketing agencies focus on 4 common 'Ps' that help them guide their activities. These 4 'Ps' are: product, place, promotion and price. At WAM, we take a different approach, and we'll use this approach to help you build your marketing strategy. Our 4 'Ps' are: People, Passion, Pioneering and Purple. This book has been divided up into 4 sections which in turn reflect our four 'Ps.'

* In the **People** section we'll be addressing the aspect of marketing that is all about relationships. You see, relationships create a foundation for your marketing. If you don't adequately understand them or address them well enough you'll just be flinging messages at the wall, hoping something sticks. Sometimes something will stick, of course—throw enough at the wall and something always does. But you'll never reach your true potential.

What kinds of relationships are we talking about?

First, there's the relationship between you and your business. The way that you understand and perceive your business is incredibly important to your overall marketing success.

Believe it or not, most people get this wrong, because they decide what their business *should* be and start marketing from that direction, instead of identifying what their business actually *is*. This isn't entirely surprising. A business identity flows from your personal identity, and few people are comfortable being exactly who and what they are without at least a little coaxing.

Next, there's the relationship between your business and your customers; and your business and your community. A lot depends on how you present these relationships, and how customers *perceive* these relationships. If you don't do a good job of understanding them then your marketing message won't be congruent with what you're actually doing and you'll create a jarring experience which will undermine your efforts at building a loyal group of repeat customers. Furthermore, you'll waste time and money talking to people who are never going to listen to you.

Next, we have the **Passion** section. At WAM we're passionate about each of our clients and we carry that passion into everything we do.

Hopefully you started your business because you were passionate about something, too! To an extent, marketing is all about doing what it takes to effectively communicate that passion to other people.

So in this section, we'll show you exactly how to share your passion with the right people.

We'll teach you how to articulate that passion in a way that is clear not only to you but to everyone else. And we'll help you identify the audience that you're most passionate about serving and working with, so that you can focus your efforts on talking to those people—and only those people.

In the **Pioneering** section we're going to give you a roadmap for really building and launching your strategy. Why 'pioneering?' It's not just to fit our 4 Ps! You're going to have to stay creative and flexible as you market your business. Sometimes you'll even have to do some trail blazing. And just like any pioneer or trailblazer, you're going to need a map of the terrain. You're also going to need to know what to do when you face the unexpected. We're going to give you those tools right here.

* Finally, there's the **Purple!** We *love* purple at WAM because it impacts the body, the mind and the spirit.

It also stands out, and that's why we only use purple in our branding. It's fun! It grabs your attention and lets you know that something special is going on. In this section, we'll be talking about how to get *your* body, mind and spirit on track so that you can programme yourself for success and so that you can have *fun* with your marketing… even if you believe 'fun' and 'marketing' should never take up space in the same sentence ever again.

By the time you're done reading, marketing and the activities associated with marketing should no longer feel intimidating or baffling. You'll have made the important mindset shifts necessary to give your business its best chance of fulfilling your vision for your company and for your own future. In fact, this may be the **most important book that you read this year**!

Proven Strategies for Success

Chapter One

People

Define your way

A brand is not a logo

Defining your brand

One very important reason why your brand is so key to your success

Part 1: People

How do you get strategic about marketing? You start by adopting a mindset that supports your marketing and your business. This means that you may have to shift some of your assumptions. You have to shift assumptions about what it means to be in business in the first place. You have to shift your assumptions about what you can and can't do, and about what you can and can't afford. You have to shift your assumptions about what marketing means. I'm going to challenge you to question some assumptions throughout the course of this book but I promise it's for your own good.

You also have to get a bit analytical. You have to be willing to really delve into your business. You need to ask yourself some questions and you need to be ready to act on the answers that you come up with. This can be an intensive process but it's an important one. If you don't understand your business, you can't think strategically about what your business needs.

If you can't think strategically about your business needs then you're going to wind up doing whatever seemed good to you at the time, and that's a recipe for disaster, as you will find yourself repeating actions and getting different results. Einstein actually defined insanity as doing the same thing over and over again and expecting different results.

To complete this strategic thinking you're going to have to start by understanding a series of very important relationships. As mentioned in the introduction, these are:

- The relationship between you and your business
- The relationship between your business and your customers
- The relationship between your business and your community

As you evaluate these relationships you're going to have to think about how *you* perceive these relationships, as well as how you want these relationships to *be* perceived. This in turn will impact how you craft your message: how you present yourself and introduce yourself to the people you want to form these relationships with—that is, your customers and your potential customers.

Take out a notebook and a pen. We're going to start by evaluating your business.

To do this, I'm going to ask you a series of questions. These questions are designed to help you really get to know your business so that you can start making decisions about it. By the time you've finished answering these questions you should have a clearer picture of what your business is and how it functions. Some of these may seem a little bit basic, but answer them anyway. The idea behind this exercise is to be truly mindful about your business.

1. **What does your business do or sell/what kind of value does it provide to others?**
2. **Who does your business serve?**
3. **What kinds of problems do these target customers share?**
4. **What does it take to make your business work?**

    a. Ordering stock/supplies
    b. Servicing customers, if you're a service business
    c. Developing a brand
    d. Marketing your business
    e. Designing and updating your website
    f. If you have a physical shop: keeping it clean and tidy
    g. Sales
    h. Paying the bills
    i. Collecting and issuing invoices
    j. Performing routine customer service
    k. Other? (Write anything else you can think of here).

Define your why

Your 'why' is the cornerstone of **your relationship to your business.** Defining and understanding this relationship is a powerful step that you must take before you can really proceed. This is going to tell you a lot about how you're going to allocate your energies. It's also going to tell you what you, personally, bring to this business.

Here's another question for your notebook:

5. Why did you start your business in the first place?

I've set this question aside by itself because it's one of the most important questions that you can answer. It's so important that it deserves its very own section.

The answer is probably because you have a skill, and hopefully a passion that you want to share with the rest of the world, but it could be something different. After all, everyone's 'why' is different! People who buy car washes don't necessarily have a burning passion for washing cars or some sort of inborn car wash skill. You might have purchased a car washing business because you wanted a time-honoured, tested business which could make money even when you weren't there.

Your 'why' might then be simply because you wanted more time with your family.

In my experience, having a strong 'why' can mean the difference between success and failure. When you have a strong 'why', you're ready to spring out of bed in the mornings. You can face the day, even if your business isn't performing just as you want it to just yet. You are also more excited about sharing your business with others. Talking about it just comes naturally.

* If your 'why' is strong enough the 'how' will unfold as you go along. This is an important insight. You see, some people make a deadly mistake when they start a new business. They start thinking they need to acquire lots of new **skills**. They think they suddenly have to become expert marketers or expert accountants. In truth, there are already plenty of people out there who have these skills. They can do that job for you, if you let them. That way, you can get on with what you are good at.

You need to be ruthless in your approach to your time. Go back to Question #4 in the exercise you've just completed. Go through this list of tasks with a pen. As you do this, ask yourself: "Am I the best person to perform that role?"

If the answer is, “no” then make a clever investment in your business success. Find out who *is* the best person to perform that role, and pay them to do it for you. If the answer is yes, then circle the task, that’s what *you* need to be doing!

You may not be 100% sure whether or not you are the right person to complete a role yet. That’s okay, and you may learn about that role and change your mind later. Just remember that you should reserve most of your time for the practice of your primary skill or passion. That is absolutely where all of your money is.

Think about it, a surgeon doesn’t spend time writing blog posts for his business. He’s busy performing surgery! He gets paid a lot of money to perform that surgery, too. He hires a marketing manager instead. He never sets his own appointments. He has a receptionist or an office manager to do that for him. If he were busy setting appointments he’d never have time to perform surgery and his practice would fold just like that. The surgeon is going to succeed by *being a surgeon.*

If you're not sure that you actually included everything in the list just keep in mind that most business tasks can be broken up into 1 of 5 functions:

- **Marketing** the product or service—getting the word out.
- **Selling** the product or service—getting into direct contact with your customer and closing sales.
- **Servicing** the customer—fulfilling the order, whether you're boxing up a product and sending it off or actually performing a service. This would also include any routine customer service, like addressing customer problems, technical issues or complaints.
- **Accounting**—dealing with the money, from taking in what the customer owes you to paying out what you owe to other people.
- **Operations**—this includes any function that keeps your business going, such as ordering supplies, ordering stock, cleaning your office or shop.

The way these different tasks look varies from business to business. If you're selling private jets to wealthy playboys, your sales function is going to be very complex - it will require a high degree of expertise, charisma and skill at business development - you'll also have a very long sales cycle.

People only buy and replace private jets every so often and they usually take a long time to make their decision.

If you're selling pies at the corner shop it requires a cashier who can ring up the pies. You could give the job to someone without any particular expertise. Sales cycles will also be very short… someone might well buy multiple pies each week, or each month. The decision-making process is different too. Pies are likely to be an impulse purchase or a gift purchase. A private jet is likely to be a purchase that requires a great deal of thought and attention on the part of the purchaser. The private jet salesperson may expect to field a lot of questions or objections. The cashier may only need to ask, "Do you want gravy with that?"

These different business functions overlap, too. The cashier who rings up the pies will probably turn around and bag them up for the customer a few seconds later, which means she's moving effortlessly from the 'selling' role to the 'servicing' role. In this hypothetical pie business it might not be efficient to have a second employee whose *only* job is serving up the pies.

Some people are better at some roles than others. Accountants are probably not at their most comfortable if placed in a sales role, for example.

Accountants are usually happiest when they are sitting at their desk, accounting. They don't want to get out there and deal with people. Accountants are intelligent people, so they can figure out how to do it if they have to, but they'll never put the energy, drive and focus into that role that they put into the accounting side of their business.

That's why most successful businesses hire at least a few employees or outsource at least a few functions. You can simply accomplish more by playing to your strengths. You can make more money by leveraging other people's time and expertise.

Now I can already hear you groaning. You're probably saying, "Oh yes. Right. I've barely even started yet. How can I afford to hire *anyone* to take on *any* of these functions?"

I'm here to ask you "Can you afford *not* to?" Your business needs its best start out of the gate, and by choosing to take on tasks that other people can handle better you're choosing to handicap it. For example, let's talk about accounting. Unless you are opening up an accountancy business you are probably not an accountant. If you choose to try to do it all on your own just because you think an accounting program can do the job 'well enough' your business might find itself paying money out in taxes that an accountant could have saved you. In the end paying an accountant would have been cheaper.

If you have a business where you issue invoices, believe me when I say, the money you would pay to a book keeper will be far less than the money you could have earned in the time it takes you to produce, send out and chase all your invoices.

What about servicing the customer? Maybe you started a cleaning business because you're really good at cleaning, and you truly enjoy it. If you never hire any other cleaners (people to fill the service role) then your income is always going to be limited by your own time. Instead, you could be spending time using your cleaning expertise to develop a standardised approach that every person in your business will be following, which means you can teach staff how to do the job while you focus on making sales. Then you could have as many clients as you want, without worrying about whether or not you have time to serve them. Of course, you would only do this if you decided your true talent was selling the business; if it's not, you might need to hire a sales rep instead.

If you never hire a sales rep or hire someone else to serve the customer you will always be dividing your time between meeting with customers as a professional business owner and scrubbing their toilets...two roles which might not ultimately work together very well. Furthermore you will never be as productive and you'll never accomplish as much because you'll constantly have to switch gears in order to wear these two vastly different hats.

Every business owner will have to answer these questions differently because every business is different. But every business owner will ultimately have to decide how and where they're going to spend their energy.

If your talent is as big as your 'why' then your time is best spent doing whatever it is that you are good at. Believe me, you will be able to earn more doing what you are good at than anything else. If you're not starting a marketing firm then this probably isn't marketing. If you want to be a designer, for example, then you need to spend your time designing things for clients. You need to let a marketing firm let the world know that you exist so you can have clients to design things for. You'll get more clients than you would have got on your own and you'll probably be a lot more comfortable and a lot happier too. After all, if you're not a marketer, you probably aren't going to enjoy marketing as much as concentrating on the area where your skills lie.

Now, some people might say, 'Well, I'm good at all of these things." Maybe that's true. Maybe you're a very rare, very talented individual who actually can perform all of these business functions without a hitch. But how happy will you be?

Choosing to take on all of these business roles means working 80 hours a week or more.

It means courting burnout and never seeing your family—which might be ironic, since many small business owners start their own businesses because they hope to see *more* of their families. Soon the amount of stress that you are undertaking will lead straight to burnout and disillusionment with the business. Some businesses don't fail because they run out of money. Some fail because the owners try to do everything and they get too tired to continue. You have limited resources: time, money, personal energy and drive so use them wisely!

What about the money? There has been a whole trend lately in which people are told that they can start a business for practically nothing. It's true. You can *start* a business for practically nothing but you're asking the wrong question if you're asking "Can I start a business?"

Anyone can **start** a business. But we already know that most people can't **stay** in business. They can't keep their doors open and that's the real question.

Not "Can I start a business?" but "Can I keep a business?" I recommend getting out of the 'start a business for nothing' mind set. This doesn't mean that you necessarily need hundreds or thousands of pounds to start a business. I would advise you to write out all of the tasks that will need doing in your business. Then get on the phone and start calling around.

Find out what it costs to have other people doing the work for you. I think you will get a pleasant surprise. Don't guess and assume, call and ask!

Once you have these answers, commit to saving up enough to pay these professionals for 6 months. They will pay for themselves many times over when they are doing your book keeping and tax returns correctly, presenting you with a beautiful website, bringing you clients, or anything else you need. You'll be happier and less stressed because you'll be following your 'why' instead of trying to wear every hat that your business plan might require. You'll make more sales too because you will look, feel and act more professional.

So, to recap, understanding your 'why' is the key to creating a healthy, happy relationship with your business. And since your business identity can only flow from *you:* from your heart, mind-set and personality—this is vital. If your relationship with your business is dysfunctional then your business will be dysfunctional.

If you are unhappy or overwhelmed, you'll start making mistakes, which will impact the way that your business is perceived. This can destroy your confidence if you're not careful. The one thing it will definitely do is have a negative impact on your income.

I'm not here to tell you whether you're the best person to handle your accounting or your customer service, only you can do that. However, by the time you've finished reading this book hopefully you will have worked out if you are the best person to do your own marketing.

Maybe you are—some people who read this book certainly will be. If you aren't, at least you will have had time to develop a marketing strategy and will be able to communicate that strategy to whichever agency you choose to work with. Working with an agency does not mean that you're not going to be involved in the process any more. You will still have to tell them what you want and need. You will need to give them the insider knowledge of your business so they can succeed on your behalf. You will be able to articulate your business brand to the marketing agency so that the marketing agency, in turn, can articulate it to the world.

A brand is not a logo

Let's talk about one of the biggest misunderstandings in the world of marketing: the difference between a brand and a logo. Why start here? Marketing is all about communicating and building a brand. If you don't understand what a brand actually is or how to build one then you're going to have a hard time accomplishing what you want and need to accomplish. Most people believe that a brand is simply a logo, a visual representation of your business. A brand, however, is much more than that. It is an expression of your business' unique identity and personality.

Every business has a unique identity and personality. Believe it or not, many customers will come to you specifically because they *like* this personality and want to work with it. When you start digging into your brand you are truly digging into the nuts and bolts of your business' relationship with customers and your business' relationship with your community. The best marketing happens only when you communicate this personality effectively, which in turn allows you to forge these relationships in an authentic, memorable way.

What happens if you don't communicate the business personality effectively? Customers come into your shop, or hire your services and they are disappointed. They might be disappointed even if you did a great job, because their experience wasn't congruent with the promises that were made in the marketing materials. They will feel like something is 'off' and they won't build nearly as much trust or loyalty.

Why has this happened? Because your relationship has got off to a bad start. It's a little like online dating. If a 40 year old puts up a photo from when he or she was 20 years old you'd be disappointed when you met in person, even if you liked everything else about the person. You'd feel misled, and maybe like you'd had your time wasted. The relationship may recover if the date goes exceptionally well—but it probably won't, even if your date explains that this was the only photograph he or she had available to use. You probably would be left wondering why the date couldn't be bothered to take a picture that showed them as they really are.

Let me give you an example of how this might work in a business setting. Let us say that your business has an incredible air of brisk efficiency about it. You move fast. You get the job done right. There's no dallying around and no small talk.

You act this way and your employees act this way, and as such you beat deadlines. You beat them so well that you're the envy of the industry. There's nothing wrong with that business identity, and there are tonnes of very busy people who would enjoy working with a company like that.

But what if you hadn't really thought about your business identity very much when you started doing all of your marketing? What if you started advertising that your firm was all about old fashioned friendliness and service with a smile, because that is what you *think* a business like yours should be all about? What would happen when customers walked through the door? They'd be upset, because nobody's stopping to talk to them, beyond asking them what they needed. Everything's rushed; everyone is in a hurry. They expected one experience, and they got another one.

The same would be true if you actually *were* that warm, friendly, service-with-a-smile type of place, but advertised on your efficiency. Now the busy businessman is staring at his watch while you try to engage him in light conversation, and he's growing more impatient because he just wants to run in and run out like your brochure or your website indicated he could.

You can only create this congruent experience if you've really stopped to think about your unique business identity. You're not just hanging a sign over a door and saying, "Come and buy my things, which are basically just like everyone else's things, but cheaper." No! If you did that you'd be out of business in a few months, because you'll only ever be able to compete on price, and someone can *always* afford to offer a better price than you. In my experience competing on price never works as once you have done it you have nowhere else to go.

What you need to be saying is, "Working with me is something **special**. I'm going to meet your needs as never before, and I'm going to do it because my work is different than anything you've ever experienced in the past. I'm going to be able to do this because you and I are compatible, and I understand you as nobody else can. We're compatible because my business has this unique personality that fits with who and what you are and who and what you need."

This unique personality is your *brand*, and the minute you started your own business your brand started to develop. It's already a part of your business. You need to understand it and manage the development of it. By now you may be feeling just a little bit confused. If a brand is not a logo, then what is a logo?

Why do businesses spend hundreds of pounds designing custom made logos? Why do businesses sue other businesses if Business A creates a logo that looks too much like Business B's logo?

It's a good question, and I'm not trying to indicate that a logo isn't a valuable business asset. A logo does gain value as the brand gains value. Let me explain. **A logo is just an image that evokes or represents the brand.** The Nike logo doesn't help Nike succeed because it's just so pretty. The Nike logo is effective because Nike has spent a lot of time helping to build the associations between certain feelings—that is, the feelings evoked by the brand—and their logo. Now when you see that logo, consciously or unconsciously, you feel all of those feelings. The logo does an effective job of representing the Nike brand.

If you don't really have strong branding then your logo really doesn't mean anything. It won't create the same associations in the mind of the customer. It will just be a really pretty picture. Your brand is your business identity, your unique business personality. When we speak of building a brand we're not speaking of *creating* that personality, because you can't create it. Your business personality is already there, playing itself out in every single interaction with every single customer, day in, day out.

Instead, when we speak of 'building a brand', we're speaking of the process of communicating that brand until everyone who comes across your business understands what your business is about.

You can do without a logo, at least in the first few weeks. You *cannot* do without a well-understood and well-articulated brand. You *must* know what you're about, and you *can't* stop communicating what you're about, ever. You must ruthlessly quash any business activity which runs counter to what you're all about, and you must not engage in any new activity which might threaten the integrity of what you're all about. This is what it means to build a brand. You're going to play to your business' strengths, and you're going to play them to the hilt. I don't mean that you're never going to *improve* your business, because you are. But you're also not going to waste any time trying to be all things to all people.

In spite of these important distinctions, many start-ups run out and create a logo first. They feel like everything will be great if they can just get the logo right. As such, they'll spend more money on a logo than they'll spend on any other business expense, even if they believe they haven't got enough money to hire an accountant, a solicitor or a marketing agency. To the mind of the novice business owner, all successful businesses have logos, and therefore logos have to come first.

But logos don't sell products. Think about it, have you ever run out and bought anything because a company's logo was just so beautiful? Of course you haven't. If a company convinces you that they can solve your problem like nobody else possibly can, do you even care whether or not they have a logo? No. You care about whether or not they can actually solve your problem. On a subconscious level, you may care about whether or not they presented themselves in a congruent fashion: whether or not their advertising personality matched up with the business personality you experienced when you walked in the door.

So don't commission a logo to be developed until you have ascertained what your business is about. If you do, your logo won't really match your business personality. Once you start using a logo it's not an easy thing to change because you've started to associate your logo with your company.

How mismatched could a brand and a logo get? Well, let's think about someone whose graphic designer gave them a red, spiky logo. It might have been really visually appealing to you because you simply like the colour red. But the whole logo looks very powerful and aggressive. That's great if your brand is also powerful and aggressive.

But if you're actually a very warm, nurturing company then you've created a big clash. How many nursing homes or day care centres do you see with red, aggressive, spiky, futuristic logos? You won't see too many, because the feelings invoked by such a logo might not inspire the paying customers to leave their mother or father or toddler with those caregivers. Conversely, you won't see many successful punk rock stores sporting pink fluffy logos featuring balloons and stuffed bears. When you finally decide on a logo you want it to evoke emotions that build and support the things that your business already conveys and accomplishes.

You may now be starting to get scared. You may be wondering if your business is *really* all that different or special. After all, you might not have given any of this any thought when you hung your signage. You were just thinking that you loved web design and were good at it, and so opened up a web design company. Or you were thinking that you love kids, and so opened up an in-home day care. You can't think of a single thing which might indicate that you have a brand at all!

Take a deep breath, I guarantee that your business *is special* and it *is unique.* As you'll soon see, it's actually impossible for any two businesses to be anything *but* unique. You just have to get to know your business a little bit.

People

Once you do, the differences between you and other companies will come shining through.

As I take you through the following exercises you will gain an intimate understanding of what makes your business great. You'll have absolutely no problem communicating that understanding to the rest of the world, whether you're doing so in marketing materials that you put together yourself—or in a creative brief that you're sharing with a marketing agency who is going to handle the technical side of marketing on your behalf.

For those of you who have been in business a while and now realise that the logo and the brand are not working, don't worry, it is not too late to change things. Over the years we have successfully rebranded lots of companies who had a logo that didn't work with a brand that had been developed over time. On those occasions we have developed a new logo that fit with the overall branding of the company.

Defining your brand

Let's add another question to the list that's growing in your notebook.

6. How does your business do things differently?

Write this question down even if you currently think that there isn't anything particularly new or different about your business. As we've already seen there are many different reasons why people start their own business. Understanding why is also the first step to understanding how your business does things differently. For example, does it offer a new service or correct a problem?

Unless your product or service is 100% brand new you're going to have competitors. By new I don't mean the date you opened your doors. By this, I mean that it's a new technology or method of doing things that has never been seen before. Even MySpace, one of the very first top social media sites, had competitors. It had e-mail, snail mail, and even other forms of entertainment. It wasn't the only social media site, but it served two primary purposes: communication and entertainment. There were still plenty of old fashioned ways to achieve other ends.

These were indirect competitors, but they were still competitors. Of course, before long, other social media sites hit the scene. MySpace hadn't really bothered to create a brand beyond, "We're a social media site," and so it was pushed out. So *how* was it pushed out? Well, other sites such as LinkedIn, Facebook and Twitter emerged onto the social networking scene with individual USPs, so users could use the sites with a specific motive in mind. For example, LinkedIn was designed for industry professionals, who wanted to network online with other likeminded professionals.

When you were thinking about starting your business maybe there was something that bugged you and you wanted to find a solution. If you started your business to provide a solution then you have already got a great start for your brand. It's easy for you to answer what you do differently, even if you don't yet have a handle on who you are.

If you don't fall into either category you've got a bit of work ahead of you. You may be a business owner who just started the business without stopping to give these deeper issues a moment's thought. Loving what you do *is* a valid reason to start a business but if you want to create an effective marketing strategy you can't stay in that place. You have to dig a little deeper and decide how you are different.

The answers are going to lie somewhere in **your** personality.

Why your personality? Remember, this is all about relationships. Business is people, and you are at the centre of your business. Your own personality is going to radiate out into the business. Your personality defines the business personality. It cannot do anything else. To demonstrate this point let's imagine two pet sitting firms and two fictional business owners. Lucy Lucky and Peter Pelley both started their pet sitting firms because they really love pets. We're going to assume both of them are very competent people and they both do a very good job. However, they are never going to be able to create the very same business, even though they offer the very same service.

Why? Lucy Lucky of Lucky's Pets is the kind of person who is highly organised. She's into brisk efficiency and she's very tech savvy. Her website offers online tools for scheduling a sitter, submitting instructions on pet care and paying bills. She's developed a mobile app to allow customers to do the same thing and once she hires a few more sitters she hopes to allow customers to use the app or the site to schedule fast service in as little as an hour. This is who she is... she's a busy, capable person who would rather use a computer than talk to a live human being over the phone. She's still warm and caring with the pets but she's also developed a very strict, standardised schedule.

She can actually hand that schedule out to new customers so they know exactly how their pets will be treated under her care. See how her personality seeps into the business? Can you see how she'd appeal to a certain type of customer? I think Lucky's Pets would attract a lot of young professionals between the ages of 25-35; people who are going places in their careers, people who might be asked to work overtime at a moment's notice, and people who are very comfortable with technology. I think she'd be an utter turnoff for senior citizens who just want to go on holiday knowing that their beloved pets are going to be happy, safe and pampered. A nervous senior pet parent would be really put off by Lucy's brusque, efficient approach.

When Lucy starts hiring she's going to look for no-nonsense individuals who get the job done with minimum fuss. That's because *she'll* be put off should any of her interview subjects start attempting to engage her in small talk. As such, Lucy's efficiency is going to continue to permeate the business, even after she fills it with other people. Note that there's nothing *wrong* with Lucy. Her personality has many strengths. When she plays to those strengths she attracts a very specific sort of person. Attempting to attract a different sort of person (the senior pet parent) would play to her weaknesses. It's never a good idea to play to weaknesses.

You end up spending all your time and energy working on those weaknesses and you never quite turn them into strengths. At best, they become a bit less of a liability. You will never build a successful business that way.

Meanwhile, Peter Pelley starts Pete's Pet Sitting. Peter has a very different personality indeed. He's easy-going, warm and friendly. His website just says to call the business or e-mail him to set up an appointment, and when he gets to each appointment he spends a great deal of time asking about each pet's individual quirks and needs. Peter is very talented at building a rapport with customers because he's genuinely good with people. He's not that organised; he keeps a calendar and that's about it. He does like technology but his approach is a little different. He sets up Skype calls so that pet parents can interact with their dogs while they're away, or at least see how they're doing if the dog isn't keen on coming to the computer. If he can't set up a Skype call he might take a photo of the pet, healthy and happy, and send it to his client's smart phone. Peter brings a big box of toys to each appointment and spends at least 20 minutes playing with each pet. He warmly takes a photo of every pet he works with and displays each photo on his website because he honestly loves each dog and cat so very much. He can't help but think of each of his clients as friends.

When Peter decides to hire a couple more pet sitters, he's going to pick warm, friendly, sympathetic personalities who can adopt his exact approach. He would probably be horrified by someone who approached the job as a series of checkpoints, or an approach which says the goal is to maximise the number of pet visits achieved in a single day. Again, Peter's personality has infused his business. There will be variations in each of his employees—not everyone will be *as warm* as Peter—but the people who he employs will still resonate on the same frequency as Peter.

Larger corporations refer to this as their 'culture.' By the time a company is a corporation the culture has usually become well defined and has taken on a life of its own. But you can bet that the culture flowed from the original founders. It had to come from inside of their hearts and minds, even as they chose the specific words that they used to convey that culture. If you took a different group of founders from the first and placed them in the same industry they would come up with an entirely different culture than the first group. It all comes from people first.

That's not to say that Lucy will never play with pets (it is, after all, part of the job) or that Peter won't eventually add a scheduling tool to his website. But it will hardly matter either way, because they're still very different people.

Imagine for just a moment if Lucy tried to market herself by talking about her warm, caring pet care service. Her business would fall totally flat because she can't maintain that brand! She's not a bad person. She's just a Type A personality who isn't very good at small talk (maybe that's why she likes animals better than people). She is never going to convey warmth. That isn't who she is. She's never going to hire for warmth. That is not what she values.

And Peter? If he tried to convey efficiency and convenience he'd have a hard time too. He'd annoy his clients the first time he wanted to have a 20 minute conversation with them instead of letting them get out of the door. He's not driven by efficiency.

Both Lucy and Peter already have a brand, whether they recognise it or not. By understanding their unique personalities and how those personalities are shaping their brand they can be more effective as they seek to communicate their business values to other people. They can also 'play it up,' doing everything they can to make their business more of what it already is. In so doing, they'll create truly loyal customers.

Lucy's brand could be summed up as 'convenient pet care' while Peter's is, 'I treat you and your pets like you're my own family'.

What would happen if Lucy and Peter partnered up? The brand would change again and they'd have to analyse the business created by their relationship. The symmetry between them would create something totally different than the sum of its parts and they'd have to be very honest and very perceptive to convey the difference to others.

There is no sense in trying to force your business into being something it's not. You can always improve how you do things, but your business personality will always shine through. It *should* always shine through. It needs to be distinct. Customers need to feel it from the moment they start interacting with you. It will impact everything you do moving forward, from the colours you select, to the copy you write, to the channels you choose to adopt in order to spread your message. Lucy might want a lively black, white and blue website to convey the efficiency and convenience. Peter might want something in soft greens, with lots of photos. Black, white and blue won't work for Peter; it would appear to be too clinical.

So who are you? How do you do business? Think about your personality and how your personality impacts the business. You can think about both positive and negative qualities. If you're really impatient then you might well have created a business with really fast turnaround times.

Why? You don't want to wait, so you're not about to make your clients wait for stuff either. If you're an aesthetic person you might have focused heavily on the sensory aspect of your offerings. Maybe you're the only cleaning service in town that offers a free aromatic soy candle, which you light when you've finished cleaning because you want to turn that nice, clean house into a sensory experience for your customers.

Think about the way you view your business and the way you offer services to your customers. Think about what you want them to feel, or see. Why do you want them to feel that way? Why do you want them to see this specific thing? Are you actually making that happen? Could you do more to really bring that experience home?

This exercise offers you some chances to create an even better experience for your customers. Our aesthetic cleaner might only have been thinking about certain things, like the smell of her lemony organic cleaning solution as it infused the whole house, the gleam of freshly polished hardwood floors and the sense of calm that descends over the house when she's done working in it. The soy candle idea might pop into her head only after she's *really* understood how *she* views the value she provides to other people.

This, too, is building your brand: coming up with ways to make it even better by adjusting your product or service to be a better fit for the business personality that already exists.

Be sure to write down all of your thoughts as you work to answer Question #6. Don't censor yourself. Read through what you've written. Does it ring true? Do you feel like you've adequately captured who you are and the true nature of your business? If so, you may just have found your brand. Later, we'll take elements of what you have written and work with them to create a concise, effective and clear statement.

One very important reason why your brand is so key to your success

Some companies never get around to defining their brand, and as a result, they suffer. Almost all of the companies that fail within 5 years suffered from this very, very common problem. What happens to a company without a well-defined, well-understood and well-marketed brand? Such a company **has no message**. Such a company lacks any way to truly distinguish itself from the competition. Without a way to distinguish itself from the competition most business owners default to the idea that customers always want the lowest price.

That price is the only thing customers care about and so they sell on price. They try to undercut competitors. They run sales and discounts.

Their message becomes, "We've got the lowest prices—guaranteed!"

Such a company has a long, uphill battle ahead of it, because it's **always** going to be lowering its prices. Competitors will adjust their prices too and someone else—someone with a stronger brand—will always supplant the low price discount guy. Companies who choose to compete on price run on the world's largest hamster wheel. That's probably why these companies' advertisements always sound so frantic and desperate.

One of two things will happen to any company that sells on price. The first is that the company could stay in business but it will have to do increasingly unethical things to keep its prices low. The company will have to cut corners; buy shoddy goods, cut wages and benefits to a bare minimum (if it has employees), work so fast that quality suffers, source goods from sweat shops and make other such compromises. Some of these compromises might actually put people's lives and health at risk. Some may just result in a shoddy product that doesn't really solve problems.

Sooner or later people will get the idea that the low cost doesn't represent good value and the company's reputation will suffer. Some people will still go to the company anyway because many people have very tight budgets.
If you've only got £20 and you need shoes then you're going to go to the one guy in town who sells shoes for £20, even if you already know that those shoes are going to fall apart in a few months. But I'm sure that particular shoe shopper knows that they're doing business with a substandard company... and they'd go elsewhere if they could.

Unless you are a sociopath, you will not be happy running that kind of company. All of your passion will be sucked away from you. The regular diet of negative feedback that you receive from the customers, who suffered at the hands of your cut corners and shoddy processes, will start to wear on your soul. You'll probably end up selling the business quickly and you won't make much on the sale. After all, you'll have to sell the business itself on price. This often translates into a sale of furniture, fixtures and equipment because the business identity or process itself simply has no value. All of your hard work, sweat and tears will have been for nothing.

If you don't compromise your integrity the business will simply fold. Sooner or later you will reach a point where you can't cut prices anymore without taking a loss on your business year after year. You either will not be able to pay your bills because you keep cutting costs anyway, or you'll have to stop—and a bigger competitor with a stronger brand and a lot more wriggle room will effortlessly undercut you.

Without even the promise of price to sell on, your business will close its doors and you'll be left with all of the debts and disappointments.

I suspect that a high percentage of the 95% who don't make it will have resorted to selling on price. I am not saying you can't offer a good, solid, fair, reasonable price for your goods or services. If you can deliver a service both fast *and* well, for example, then you may well be able to afford to charge less money for that service because you can service two clients in the time it takes most of your competitors to service one. That's just a competitive advantage that's part of your brand. You just don't want to make the price your one and only selling point. You want your customer to say, "ABC Company's services were so good, the owner was great, the company did a little bit extra, *and* the price was really great, too." Having a strong brand will absolutely save you, even if you just have no way of competing on price. Because making the choice to do business with your company becomes about more than price.

A carpenter can't compete on price with a large furniture company. Instead the carpenter has to compete on the unique handmade pieces he creates; the high quality of the finished product, the sensory pleasures of the look and feel of the piece he has created.

His brand has to be about quality and prestige and whatever else he brings to the table... almost to the point where his customers feel *pride* in their ability to pay a lot more to get something a lot better. Your brand may well fit that category.

You can only make good decisions about the role that prices will play in your business after taking the time to truly understand your brand. If you're going to take the extra time to check over everything you do, then you have to charge a bit more and emphasise price a bit less. If you're focusing on efficiency then you might charge less because you can do more with your time—or you might charge *more* because you offer rush jobs. You have to use your understanding of your brand to position all aspects of your offering.

The same goes for any features that you offer. A bed and breakfast that's going for a warm, homelike atmosphere can probably get a lot of traction out of offering a free warm homemade cookie each time a customer walks through the door.

The IT support company that puts a plate of warm homemade cookies out on the receptionist's desk won't quite have the same impact. A visitor may enjoy the cookie but it's not going to do a thing for the company. They might as well save the money they'd be spending on those cookies and use it for something else. Their brand will revolve around delivering results and cookies don't say a thing about results!

Then again, if they're branding themselves as a fun, quirky company then cookies, iced to look like pie charts, just might be their thing. It will depend entirely on the business' personality. What works for one business isn't necessarily going to work for another because these decisions must be made in a way that aligns with the business' core personality. Taking the time to truly understand the core personality of your business may be the most important way that you could use your time on behalf of your business, even if you don't get anything else done during the course of a full week because you're working on this, and this alone. You'll need all of these notes, because in Part 2, we're going to define and refine your passion even further, turning it into a laser-focused statement that will guide all of your marketing communications as you move forward into the future.

Keep your business notebook handy. You've got more writing to do!

I've included the full list of questions that you should have answered in Part 1 in the handy one page guide listed below. If you haven't answered all of the questions yet please take a moment to do so. You will need the insights provided by many of these questions to make decisions as we move forward.

Business notebook questions

For your reference, here are all of the questions that you should have written and answered in your little notebook before you start on Part 2.

1. **What does your business do or sell? What kind of value does it provide to others?**
2. **Who does your business serve?**
3. **What kinds of problems do these target customers share?**
4. **What does it take to make your business work?**
    a. Ordering stock/supplies
    b. Servicing customers, if you're a service business
    c. Developing a brand
    d. Marketing your business
    e. Designing and updating your website
    f. If you have a physical store: keeping it clean and tidy
    g. Sales

h. Paying the bills
i. Collecting and issuing invoices
j. Performing routine customer service
k. Other? (Write anything else you can think of here).

5. Why did you start your business in the first place?

6. How does your business do things differently?

Proven Strategies for Success

Chapter Two

Passion

Defining the product and service:

The Business Summary

'X' Solution: What your business does

People with 'Y' problems: Defining your target market

'Z' Way: How you do things differently

Clarify your communication

Part 2: Passion

Are you really excited about your business, its mission, and the value that it can bring to other people? If so, then you can stop thinking about *marketing* and start thinking about sharing your passion with the world!

Of course, not everyone is ready to hear your message. There are plenty of people who don't want to hear it because they don't *need* to hear it. Bachelors don't need to hear about products designed to help new Mums. New Mums probably don't want to hear about the latest luxury sports car (though there are always exceptions).

No, we want you to communicate to the people who have the best chance of 'getting' you. So in Part 2 we're going to help you really define your products and services. Then we're going to spend some time talking about the people who get you. That's your target market, and you're really going to reach out and talk to them.

You're going to do so feeling confident that you're reaching the right people in the right way. When you have this confidence, marketing is no longer a frightening thing.

After all, few people are frightened to talk to a stranger if they've had a proper introduction first. Few people are frightened to talk to anyone when they've identified a reason to do so.

Think about it. **If you were standing out in the middle of a crowded field on a hot day you probably wouldn't feel too shy or self-conscious about yelling that you've got ice cold bottled water for sale**. You know that this is information that your current audience desperately needs and wants. It's also no surprise to you when a good proportion of those hot, thirsty people takes the time to come over and purchase a drink. The drink is going to solve their biggest problem right now, so why wouldn't they?

The passion section will really help you 'zap' your fears about putting yourself and your business out there because identifying your target market and giving them a message that might interest them is like receiving that warm, helpful introduction from a friend. At that point you're just having a conversation, and **it's a conversation that will interest your listeners intensely.** *

Defining the product and service: The Business Summary

You've already written down some thoughts about what your business is and what it does. This may have even felt a little bit silly because the answer to the question might have been pretty obvious in your mind. If you sell widgets, then you wrote, "I sell widgets." But "I sell widgets" does not help you define your product or service in a way that creates an effective marketing strategy.

You've also taken the time to define how you do your business a little bit differently. This time, you might have written a long bullet-point list or paragraph which talks about all of the virtues of what you do. This is great information, but it's also a bit too much information right now. You might use all of it to write a web page, sales letter or brochure, but for the time being it's just not doing a good job of helping you nail down that core message; the true brand that you're going to communicate to the rest of the world.

What you need is a definitive tool which will help you tell anyone what your business does in 15 seconds or less.

This tool is known by a whole variety of names, including 'elevator pitch' and 'elevator speech', and you're about to write one. Writing a summary is relatively simple; you're going to write a sentence or two which will basically say: My business offers **X solution** to **people with Y problem** in **Z way.**

It's a very simple equation and we're going to do it step by step. At that point, you'll have a succinct, simple statement which conveys your brand and which guides all of the messaging that you're going to put together in the future. If you choose to work with someone else to do your marketing for you then you will be able to use this sentence to make sure that they understand your business.

Do not skip this step. It may seem a little simple to you, but when you finish going through the exercise you're going to have an 'Ah Ha!' moment. Many of the questions you've already written down in your notebook have been leading up to this moment. When your pitch has been written, you'll have a *very* satisfying moment when you think: *yes, **this** is how I need to communicate my business.*

You can use this summary in all sorts of places. It makes a good elevator pitch at a networking event. It may make a good tagline under a headline. It is the thing that you want most people thinking, consciously or unconsciously, when they finally see that beautifully designed logo of yours. It should really capture your passion, so that you can deliver it with a smile on your face.

'X' Solution: What your business does

It's not enough to just say, "My business sells flowers" or "My business sells pet sitting services." Flowers and pet sitting are products and services. Products and services are *not* solutions; they're just products and services. Nobody hires someone if they don't have a problem to solve and nobody buys a product that isn't going to make their life easier in some way. So you need to move past the basic item, such as flowers. Instead, you need to focus on why that item matters. Why do we *care* about your flowers? Why do we *need* your pet sitting services?

If you decide to do your own marketing, you'll come across a copywriting maxim that says, "Always focus on benefits, not features." A flower is a feature. Romance, however, is a benefit. Pet sitting is a feature. Convenient pet sitting offers a benefit. You can still use the words 'flowers' or 'pet sitting' in your summary or pitch, but they will need the addition of a benefit adjective to help nail down the real solution that you are offering. Remember, *loving pet care* is not quite the same thing as *convenient pet sitting*.

Romantic flower arrangements are not quite the same thing as *avant-garde artistic flower arrangements.* You're going for romance or convenience or avant-garde when you write the 'x solution' part of your summary.

You can do this by **thinking about what people are trying to accomplish by coming to your business**. It could be peace of mind, so they can go on holiday with a clear conscience; a cure for boredom; something to help them commemorate an event; or a cleaner house? Think about the solutions indicated by these 'X solution' examples:

- Affordable pet care - What's the problem? Pet care is usually very expensive.
- Professional web sites - What's the problem?
  Some business owners let their nieces, nephews or grandchildren make their websites, often with disastrous results.
- Romantic flower arrangements - What's the problem? You want to get the girl!
- Stress-free wedding planning - What's the problem? Planning a wedding is often a stressful, painful, emotionally fraught process. Unique local beers and cheeses - What's the problem? Some people are fed up of mass-produced beer and cheese.

Do you see the pattern here? By getting descriptive with your products and services you start to hint at all of the reasons why these products and services are actually important to people who might need or want them.
You need a descriptive phrase that paints a vivid picture, one that helps bring the problem to mind even as it offers a solution to that problem.

Your words are going to show the way your product or service makes life better for the person using it. Remember, this problem-solution statement must flow from who you are. If you are stuck ask, "What's the problem?" and work backwards from there.

Don't say your flowers are all about romance if *you're* not all about romance. If you're not, it might be better to focus on elegance instead. Perhaps when you opened your flower shop business you envisioned putting together beautiful centrepieces for people's tables.

The romance-focused person was thinking about selling flowers that would be given to someone's partner on a romantic occasion. These are two different people in the same niche offering two vastly different business products.

Remember, Peter is offering loving pet care (his X solution) and Lucy is offering convenient, modern pet care (her X solution). Without these adjectives you're just selling yet another me-too product in a crowded marketplace. That leaves you back at square one where you're forced to compete on price and that's exactly where you do not want to be.

People with 'Y' problem: Defining your target market

Once you're comfortable with your business personality, I want you to take a moment to go back to Question #2 on your worksheet:

Who does your business serve?

If you're like most people you probably put something really general here. For example, if Lucy or Peter had filled out the questionnaire with you they probably would have both written 'pet owners'. But when you solve for 'Y problem' you're going to have to think about some very specific people.

Fortunately, you've already spent some time defining the problem while coming up with your 'X solution'. Keep that problem fixed in your mind as you start trying to write your 'person with y problem' statement.

Lucy will need to write something like, Young, busy, professional pet owners. This may be easy for her, as this may have been exactly who she was thinking of when she started her business. On the other hand, she may have to think about it by asking herself who *needs* her brand.

Peter's 'people with y problems' is probably something like, Anxious pet owners who feel really guilty about going off on holiday without their pets.

That is probably a bit direct though, so he might say something like, "Pete's Pet Sitting provides **a loving home-from-home experience for your pet** (x solution) **so you can enjoy your holiday knowing they are loved and cared for** (people with y problem).

'People who feel guilty' about leaving their pets behind is implied here. After all, you want to make this statement roll right off the tongue and you want to make it appealing to potential customers.

That means you can't create a statement that embarrasses or shames your target market in any way. I've got to stress this here. Notice how Lucy's market is **not** *all pet owners.* Peter's market is *also* **not** *all pet owners.*

There may well be some overlap between their customer bases. There may be people out there who would be equally happy using Lucy or using Peter, and might call the other when one isn't available. But for the most part Lucy is talking to a very specific segment of pet owners, and so is Peter.

There are also a whole lot of pet owners who won't ever use either of them. There are pet owners who are happy to undergo the time and hassle of keeping a pet with them while travelling.

There are pet owners who prefer to use doggy day care so their dogs can play with other dogs when they're away. There are pet owners who are homebodies, and simply don't go anywhere at all. They may need other pet-related services, but they don't need this one.

If our friends Lucy and Peter keep trying to talk to *all pet owners* they're certainly going to waste a lot of time and energy. They're also going to waste a lot of money. They're going to write ads that say things like, "Attention pet owners!" instead of, "Are you a pet owner who is always on the go?"

Taking the time to *really* get specific about the types of people you serve offers untold advantages. It allows you to step inside very specific worlds.

It lets you speak the language of the people who live in these worlds so that they read your business' messaging and think, "That's me! This person is talking to me, and they really, really *get* me!"

Of course, nobody jumps up and says that sort of thing consciously in response to an advertisement. But they do *feel* it, at a subconscious level and the way that you make people *feel* when they do business with you is very important. If they feel like you understand them, think their problems are important and have custom-built solutions **just for them,** they'll come back again and again. You can't do this if you're trying to talk to anybody and everybody. You might still get some business, but it will never be enough business, and you'll never build any real loyalty.

Loyalty is what is going to keep *your* business alive when 95% of your entrepreneurial cohort is dropping like flies.

What can you do if you're having trouble defining your 'y people'? Perhaps you really do have a business which seems to offer something almost everyone needs.

For example, almost all retail stores need a security system. If you sell security systems you might be thinking, "No, really, I need to reach *every business owner*."

But you don't. Let's think about your ideal client; the one that you're going to want to work with day in and day out. Do you want to work with business owners who would just as soon lock the door and go home and resent the expense that your security systems represent? Of course not.

You want to work with business owners who are serious about protecting their premises and stock. You want to do business with people who understand the value in the service that you're offering. In this case, your 'x solution' might be "cutting edge security systems" and your sentence might look like this:

My business provides **cutting edge security systems** to **business owners who are serious about protecting their premises and stock.**

We haven't even got to 'in Z way' yet, but already you're setting your business apart by writing such a statement. Clear messaging is starting to emerge here. The business owner who thinks he'd rather hire someone with a dog to patrol the premises will never call you.

On the other hand the business owner, who understands that cutting edge security systems are the best way to protect their valuable assets, will respond.

Both of you will have a more pleasant experience because at that point you're not having to sell him on the value of 'cutting edge'. You're just going to *prove* that you are cutting edge and that your security systems have what it takes to protect his premises and stock.

That's a very different sales conversation, and a very different marketing conversation as well, since that is the conversation you'll be having, in theory, when you put your marketing materials together.

Some business owners are afraid to do this because they're afraid that they're going to choose the wrong hypothetical person. They're afraid that there won't be enough of their chosen person to do business with them and they're afraid that they'll be leaving money on the table.

I'm here to tell you that every marketing agency creates 'personas' for business owners to describe exactly who they will be talking to.

We call them customer avatars. We base them on real people, so in this example the avatar may be something like this: He is called Mark; he is aged between 35 and 50. He drives a Range Rover; he's in a relationship and has two children.

You don't have to work with anyone you're not passionate about helping! Business is all about adding value to people; it's about adding value to **specific** people. Perhaps when you started your business you even noticed a challenge that specific people were facing.

You noticed that nobody was offering this or that service, and even if you didn't consciously realise it at the time, this or that service appealed to a very specific subsection of the population.

If you're having trouble thinking about the person just think about the types of problems you want to solve. After all, this is the 'people with y problem' section. It's perfectly okay to define these people as 'people with y problem'. Perhaps a wedding planner would write:

My business provides **stress-free wedding planning services** (X solution) to **couples who are struggling to plan the perfect wedding** (Y problem). Again, this approach allows your target market to self-select. Is that bride struggling? No? Then she won't call you. Does she think she's struggling? Does she feel stressed out? Yes. Then she probably will.

You don't have to drive yourself mad trying to *guess* at which types of people might want to work with your business if you already know what kinds of problems you're solving.

You can just define your target market as 'people with this problem'. Stating it this way does the heavy lifting for you.

You've now taken yourself out of this realm where you're trying to talk to *all* of the people who might inhabit a certain category. You're really only talking to people who have *a specific problem*.

'Z' Way: How you do things differently

Now we'll go back to Question #6 in your notes. If you recall, the question was:

How does your business do things differently?

Again, you might have written out a whole paragraph or a series of bullet points. Now we're going to take out the most important ones and use them to finish off our concise sentence. We're going to solve for Z, and by the time we do, you're going to have real clarity within your business.

You're still going to use all of the other stuff you wrote down. After all, creating marketing communications demands a lot more than one or two sentences! However, right this second we are only concerned with nailing down your brand so that you can communicate it clearly to others.

Chances are you do multiple things well, but there are only one or two things that you do *really* well. Take out a highlighter and go through whatever you wrote. Indicate those areas where you *really* shine... the ways in which you've been known to surprise and delight people in the past.

If you built your business around offering some sort of exclusive service that nobody else was offering that's the one you're going to want to focus on. Or you simply went into business because you were good at something; you will need to define the *way* that you are good at something in order to 'solve for Z.'

Lucy's pet sitting service has no trouble solving for Z. Her full sentence might be: "My business provides **convenient pet sitting services** (X solution) to **young, busy professionals** (people with Y problem—the problem of being busy) **by offering an exclusive click-and-go scheduling service."** The key word here is 'by'. This is *how* Lucy does what she does.

Nobody else in her area allows you to simply order your pet sitting via smart phone app or via a booking form on the website.

You're going to write your own 'by' statement. *How* do you do business? *How* do you offer these products and services? *How* do you deliver the solutions which solve problems for your target audience? You do it *by* doing something extraordinary. It's time to tell us about it by finishing off your sentence.

You can end the sentence after 'people with y problem' and start a new sentence with the words, "We do this by." You're still following the formula; you're just using two sentences to do it.

It'll take the same amount of time to say it or use it. I created several sample sentences in the previous section, so I'm going to take a moment to finish them off.

I've polished a few of them a bit more, as well. I want to demonstrate what your sentence will look like when you put it all together. I want to help you understand just how powerful all of this really is. When you look at these businesses you should see a group of businesses that really have something special to offer their customers.

There are no price wars here. There is no 'me-too' marketing. There is no hype. This is just an honest statement of what makes these businesses special.

- Pete's Pet Sitting provides loving pet care which takes the guilt out of leaving your pets behind when you go on holiday. We do this by treating you and your pets like members of our own family. We offer a home-from-home experience.
- My business provides cutting edge security systems to business owners who are serious about protecting their premises and stock by creating customised, high-tech solutions to meet your individual business needs.
- My business provides stress-free wedding planning services to couples who are struggling to plan the perfect wedding. We do this by offering a catalogue of pre-planned wedding packages: simply pick the one you like and we'll do the rest!

Now it's your turn! Write your sentence and polish it up until it shines. You've just defined your offer.

You've consciously chosen the right messaging to convey your brand. You can proceed with the next step as long as you are happy you have got this part right.

If your finished statement *doesn't* ring true for you then you need to go back through the exercises. Remember, messages you use to convey your brand flow from you. Your business is, in many ways, an expression of who you are.

It expresses your personality, and it expresses how you think. A wedding planner who wants to go through every minute detail of napkin colours with a bride thinks very differently than a wedding planner who puts together 25 different themed weddings, tells a bride to "just pick one" and has developed a checklist, standardised approach to making each and every one of those weddings go off without a hitch.

Both might create some truly *wonderful* weddings but there are very different people behind those approaches. Don't be afraid to be an individual because I don't have any doubts that your business, as an expression of you, is fully capable of providing some truly wonderful, unique experiences to the people who choose to work with you.

Clarify your communication

Writing your business pitch gives you an incredible tool for guiding all of the rest of your communication messages. Every word you speak or write should flow from this single, focused statement. Every piece of graphic design that you commission or use should support that statement. The use of visual elements can be subtle and hard to pin down, but at the very least these elements shouldn't *clash* with who you are and what you do.

You also need to make sure that all of your messages are talking directly to your chosen audience. The communication needs to be about *their issues, needs and problems*, and not how great *you* are. Of course, you do have to talk about yourself a little bit, and you can: by focusing on *how* you solve problems and the *results* that you get.

For example, our hypothetical wedding planner can expand on the theme of being stressed out. She can expand on the idea that weddings come with a thousand little etiquette issues and a million different decisions. She can then explain her solution: that she's basically standardised 25 wedding packages, allowing the bride to pick the tone, theme and mood that suits her.

The planner will then simply set those wheels in motion, making the right phone calls to make that wedding happen. There are no surprises, since each wedding package comes with a pre-set price, which means the bride and groom can just budget for the specific wedding they want. She can then gather some testimonials from couples who've used her method and were wildly happy with it.

So let's say we're going to write a web page. How can we write a compelling web page with a clear marketing message that supports your brand? First, you're going to **put yourself in your ideal client's shoes.** Start by listing out all of the problems they're facing as it relates to your service or niche.

Obviously if you're selling pet sitting services you don't have to worry about how the boss is yelling at them at work or how the roof needs repairs. You *do* have to think about how more and more companies are requiring mandatory overtime, and how many of those companies choose to share this kind of information with their employees at the last possible minute. That's a big problem—how can anyone get pet sitting fast enough if they don't know they need it?

You do need to think about things this client might worry about, such as whether or not a pet sitter is going to remember to administer their dog's medication in the correct way, or whether he or she is going to arrive at the house on time.

Will the pet be sitting there, waiting and waiting, getting increasingly hungry and frantic?

One big benefit of completing this exercise is that it will allow you to think of new ways to serve your clients, ways that feed into your overall mission. This lets you improve your products or services, even as you clarify and improve your marketing messages. You can try to empathise with your target market, and that will give you a lot of material to work with.

You can do a lot just by using your imagination and thinking what their lives might be like! This is especially helpful if the target market is someone a lot like you. If you are pursuing this business because you *know, intimately* what it is like to face these problems then you can probably list out everything these people are worried about without too much trouble.

However, if you were never a member of this target group, you can't rely on your imagination alone. You need to identify other ways to find out the information. For example, you can pick up a magazine aimed at your target market and scan through the articles. Right away you're going to learn about a lot of the different problems and issues that these people face.

You're going to learn what they think about. The publication has already spent thousands of pounds trying to understand this target market. You might as well benefit from their research. You'll also learn the language used to reach your target market. This is very helpful, since speaking your client's language is a vital part of clarifying your communications. Online forums provide another good source of information. This time, you'll get the problems and issues directly from your audience.

If you're already actively serving clients then you've got a great opportunity because you can listen to the clients themselves. I like to identify the 20 most common questions and objections that clients offer to a business. I've found that in any business there are those questions and objections that you hear over, and over, and over again.

* Those things are gold dust, listen well! They tell you what's scaring your clients about doing business with you, which means you'll be able to address those fears in your communications. If you can overcome these fears and objections before they ever talk to you, you're onto a winner.

Once you're sure you really understand your target audience, it's time to start talking about their reality. You're not even going to talk about your product or service yet.

Proven Strategies for Success

You're going to talk about them. You're going to start your website off with a bang by writing a headline that speaks directly to them. It might ask them a question, make a statement about what they're facing, or give hard numbers on how you've helped people *just like them.* The headline is designed to draw attention, to entice your target audience to keep reading.

Then you're going to make your way down the page, talking about the problems they face. Be vivid, paint a picture, hit the pain points. Occasionally ask questions like, "Have you ever faced this?", "Has this ever happened to you?" The goal is to get your reader to say, "Yes! That's me! This person really gets it!"

If you do a really good job of writing about your customer's challenges, you're going to really make that customer hungry. They're going to know there's a solution coming, and they're going to want to know about it. Once you've thoroughly explored your customer's world you'll be able to gently move into your solution.

You start with your elevator pitch. You can more or less use it word for word. You can put it in bold letters if you want to. You want to draw attention to it. It's clear, it's concise, and everything else that you have to say is going to flow, effortlessly, from that single statement.

Once you've used your pitch you can start explaining your methods in a little bit more detail. You can use some of the information that you wrote in your business workbook, when you were trying to define how you are different. If you were the person who wrote all sorts of paragraphs and bullet points then you're finally going to get to share some of that information right here. I told you that you'd get to use it.

But you don't *ever* want to forget that **this is about the customer**. So you're going to aim for **evoking a feeling**. How will your customers *feel* when they get your solution? Will they feel relieved; happy; peaceful? Will there be a big smile on their face because it's just so easy? Make sure you help them feel those feelings right now.

Car salesmen have been a master of this technique for a long time. Do you think they offer test drives because they love risking their cars on the roads? Of course not, they do it because they know that it's going to be a lot harder to say no to that car once you've put yourself in the driver's seat, smelled that 'new car' smell, felt the way it holds the road and enjoyed those luxurious seats.

Unless something falls through on the financing, you're probably going to trade in your old one for a new one, it's just human nature.

So when you are writing your copy you need to elicit those good feelings. You've got to make all of this happen in the mind of your customer. You do this with vivid imagery that puts them right inside the experience you want them to have. Use sensory details, and get very specific. Of course, you could never have done this if you hadn't taken the time to understand your business well enough to know what that experience was supposed to be in the first place.

After you are happy that you have successfully created this bright new reality in the mind of your customers, it's time to show them exactly how they can move it from the inside of their heads to their real, physical, living reality. You do this with a call to action. You say, "If you want all this, click this button and order now. Pick up the phone and call me. Come to this location and visit my shop. Remember, if you do this you're going to have this wonderful experience." If you miss the call to action you've just wasted your time because nobody's going to do anything at all.

A call to action is simple. Click here. Call now. Buy now. Buy here. Visit us here. It gets people out of passive 'if only' mode and into 'I'm going to make this happen right now!' mode. This process works for *any* form of marketing communication. It works for web pages. It works for direct mail letters. It works for radio advertising.

You may lengthen or shorten the message to fit the medium but you're always going to use this same basic process to connect with your customers.

What about social media? On social media it's going to work a bit differently, since the messages are shorter and you're spending a lot of time sharing resources and engaging in conversations. In the case of social media you're going to take the approach which says, "I know my audience very well. I know what interests them and worries them. I'm going to share this relevant information, or this fun quote, or this cool picture because I know it will appeal to them."

Social media is more of a long, drawn out, ongoing conversation, than one fixed piece, and the only rule is that you must be a good host who keeps customers interested in continuing the conversation. You're still basically letting that conversation flow out of your branding message, though it may not be as obvious.

I know often when I am talking to small businesses they don't think Twitter is a tool that would work for them so I thought I would share with you some of the findings of a recent survey carried out with 1,000 active users on Twitter who were following small and medium sized businesses.

- 73% of those surveyed said they feel more positive about an SME once they have followed their Twitter accounts/ read their tweets.
- ¾ of your potential customers will look for reassurance about the credibility of your brand by searching for it on Twitter.
- 60% of those surveyed said they had purchased something from an SME due to something they saw on Twitter.
- 86% stated that they plan to purchase regularly from an SME that they follow on Twitter.

My advice would be that social media is another medium you can choose to talk to your target audience. Don't discount it without researching it to find out if your target market is on there.

Avoid Jargon!! *

In all communication you need to make sure you avoid jargon, speak clearly and plainly. There are plenty of abbreviations in every industry. I know when I worked in Education it was full of them, however, they don't necessarily mean anything whatsoever to your target market. Avoid them at all costs. If people don't understand what you are saying they won't bother asking you to explain, you will just alienate them. If you talk in terms of the benefits and results your clients get it; it's easy to understand... no jargon required.

Next, have a look and make sure you haven't written any clichéd words or phrases. A cliché is not compelling and using one is a great way to ensure that your target audience switches off. They'll sneak up on you, too. How many times have you heard phrases like, World class'; 'Best-in-class'; 'Customer-focused'; 'Experienced'; 'Professional'; 'High quality'; 'Unique'; 'Data driven'?

What do you use instead? Maybe you don't need to use anything at all. If you've used 'World class' anything, you're probably falling prey to hype. Are you *really* offering something that's *world class* or *world famous?* Instead, focus on painting the picture of what life looks like after your service or product.

A cliché is often a problem simply because it's so *vague*. What does 'experienced' mean, *exactly*? Good marketing messages are specific. That's why it's better to say, "22 years of service", instead. If you haven't been in business that long, don't worry—you'll have plenty of other selling points.

If you have specific case studies try to share them as much as possible. It's very difficult to be vague when you're telling a story about a specific instance in which a specific person was helped in a specific way. In fact, communication just doesn't get any clearer than a concrete story.

The weight loss industry has this down to a science. That's why they use 'before' and 'after' pictures. But you can use 'before' and 'after' stories, even if you don't have relevant photos. Before your customers came to you, they had problem X.

After they came to you, the problem was solved. The pain was resolved. They had a happier life as a result. It's up to you to paint that picture by choosing vivid words to describe the 'before' picture. You need equally vivid, specific words to describe the 'after' picture.

Now is a good time to 'check in' with yourself. In your earlier assessment you might have decided that you're perfectly capable of doing your own marketing. After all, marketing involves a lot of writing and you wouldn't be alone if you believed that just about anyone can write. We're all taught the technical business of writing in primary school.

Are you starting to realise that writing marketing materials is about more than knowing the correct placement of a comma? It takes a vivid imagination and the ability to convey the results of that vivid imagination to others. You have to be able to do it in a clear, concise way. If you struggled to write your elevator pitch then you're *really* going to struggle when it's time to write your marketing communications.

Talking about yourself just isn't that easy. Often, you're too close to your subject matter, even if you're the most talented writer in the world.

There are certainly shortcuts. You can look at what others have done, imitate websites you like. However, your business won't be able to put its *best* foot forward if writing marketing materials is not your strongest talent. You'll also spend far more time than you have to spend agonising over what you've written.

Do you really want to spend countless hours staring glumly at blank pages on your laptop screen when you could be out there using your talents in a way that actually supports your business? It's something to think about as we move into the next section of the book.

Proven Strategies for Success

Chapter Three

Pioneering

Selecting the media

Develop and launch a plan

Test it, monitor it and roll it out again

Part 3: Pioneering

You've done the hard work of figuring out your business brand. You've worked out who needs and wants to hear about your brand. Now you've got to develop and launch a plan for getting that message out in front of the people who are going to respond to it.

In this section I'll be showing you how to build a road map for your marketing efforts. Each step on your roadmap will achieve one very important end: building your brand as you reach your target audience. As people hear about what you do and who you help you'll grow your base of customers, which means you'll be able to stay in business.

I'll tell you about all of the different marketing channels out there. There are more than you think and you probably haven't considered all of them. While I won't give you step-by-step instructions on how to launch and manage a Facebook campaign I *will* show you how to decide whether or not that campaign is right for your business.

Proven Strategies for Success

I'll show you how to decide on the day-to-day marketing activities that you'll be tackling, if you decide that you are the best person to fulfil the marketing role in your business.

I'll also show you how to determine whether or not your marketing plan is working, so that you can make adjustments as you proceed. Marketing is all about testing and measuring, and you're going to be doing a lot of trail blazing here, which is why the 'Pioneering' label is so appropriate for what we'll be accomplishing in this section.

As I've said before, marketing demands creativity, quick thinking and focused effort. It's not always easy to see what you're doing; it can take time to know whether or not you're actually accomplishing anything. Still, you can accomplish a lot just by thinking strategically about your business and what you want your business to accomplish for you.
Let's get started!

Selecting the media

All your marketing efforts are going to take place in some form of *media*. Media is just a fancy term for a communications platform. The newspaper you read this morning is media. So is the radio station that you listened to on your way to work. Your website is media, too.

Media is broken up into a series of different 'channels'; places in which you can get your message out to your target audience. You won't use every channel that's available. Time and money generally will not allow it. However, it's still very important for you to cover a variety of different channels.

Why? Well a good marketing strategy must be robust and multi-faceted. Firstly, the role of building a brand and enticing customers relies on a series of different 'touches'. People generally won't move to do business with you the first time they hear about you. Sometimes they need to hear about you at least seven or eight times before they'll give you a try.

The first time someone hears your message they could be busy, distracted, or not have any money to spend. You have to catch them again and again. You have to fill them with the desire to do business with you so that when they *are* ready, they come to you.

Secondly, because all the people you need and want to talk to are not going to be in one place.

A percentage of them will go straight to the web but others may pay more attention to print, or radio, or television ads. You increase your chances of success by reaching more people through multiple channels. I would advocate you should be using at least ten different media channels. Failing to do this means you will not make as many sales.

It's like buying a raffle ticket. If you buy just one raffle ticket then you certainly have a chance at winning the prize. But you have a much better chance of taking home the prize if you buy fifty raffle tickets.

If that's true, why not just blast your message on every channel that exists? First, because you have limited resources, **you only have so much time** to engage with these channels and **you only have so much money to spend** on them. While many marketing methods are free, there are still a lot of them that are *not* free. So you need to select the channels that are going to give you the very best return on investment.

Second, because **some channels just aren't appropriate for some businesses**. A billboard advertisement wouldn't necessarily be the first choice for an e-commerce store. A doctor's office isn't going to do nearly as well on Facebook as a luxury resort. Your customers don't use every channel and they don't pay attention to every channel. You have to consciously select the channels that are right for your business.

Here are a few important things to consider when you select your channels:

Firstly, **do your customers use this channel?** If you're marketing outdoor adventure products, you're probably not going to spend a lot of money on placing a banner ad on a site that teaches people how to live with their heart conditions. The advert would simply be irrelevant at that point, and because it's irrelevant it will not get you any enquiries. In the same way you don't want to pay hundreds of pounds for beautiful brochures if you are not clear on how those brochures are going to get into the hands of the people who may want to buy from you.

Second, **is this channel appropriate for my type of business**? Facebook is the example that I like to use here. There's a myth that says every business needs to be on Facebook.

In truth, some businesses get great results from Facebook, particularly business to consumer companies such as, hotels, restaurants and hair and beauty salons. It is unlikely that manufacturing companies would get the same results and could use their time in better ways.

Third, **can you afford the channel?** I've already mentioned it's hard to start a business 'for free.' However, even with a start-up budget some channels will be out of your reach. Few start-ups can afford to engage in television advertising straight away, for example.

Fourth**, does this channel target the right location?** Unless you're an Internet-only business, location is going to matter. You're not going to bother advertising in Manchester if your business is based in Leeds. Most people are going to do business within a 20 km radius of their current location. You'd still use the Internet, of course (everyone's going to use the Internet in this day and age) but you're going to keep it as local as possible to increase your chances of bringing paying customers to your doorstep.

Fifth**, do your competitors use this channel?** Competitor analysis is important. There are businesses that have been succeeding in your niche longer than you have. If they are using a particular channel that is a good sign that it is working for them.

You may as well learn from their experience and save yourself lots of time and money.

You can go down the list, asking yourself all five of these questions as you evaluate the following media types. I don't suppose I will make myself very popular in the print industry when I say I am not a huge fan of advertising. It can work really well for some products and services but often people place ads with no call to action and no way of measuring its effectiveness. That to me is like pouring money down a drain.

Newspapers

Print is supposedly dead, or so they say, but I notice that people are still printing newspapers and delivering them every single day. There will be a portion of the population who prefer to have a physical paper in their hands. Newspapers can also be really local, which is great for businesses operating in a specific geographic location. There are basically two ways to market yourself in a newspaper. The first is to run an ad. If you don't have a lot of money you can stick to the classified ads, where a few lines of print might work for you. If you've got a little more to play with, you can upgrade to a display ad. Even a 1/8th page display ad (one of the smallest) can create real results if you commit to running that ad over time, with a specific call to action.

The second way to market yourself in a newspaper would be to write an advertorial. An advertorial is basically a news story. You're going to write it yourself and you're going to give it to the newspaper for free. In return, they're going to print all of your contact information so long as you've included it somewhere in the ad. This is 'guest posting' in its purest, most original form. You simply have to make sure that your story is a) actually a story and b) relevant to that section of the newspaper. You may well want to do this to position yourself as an expert in your field. You can add your phone number and business address at the end of the article.

Magazines

Magazines are still going strong. Some are local, but most serve a multitude of geographic areas. Many magazines are focused on interests, not on locations. Display ads are more expensive in glossy magazines, as you might well expect. After all, they look nicer and feel nicer! You don't have to take out a full-page display ad to reap the benefits, however. Many magazines have sections in the back where $1/16^{th}$ and $1/8^{th}$ page ads all run together.

Some magazines will take advertorials, and some won't. You can scan back issues to see if anyone else has ever run them. Generally you'll find trade magazines far more receptive to them than glossies.

Public Relations (PR)

Some people treat PR as a separate function from marketing. The truth is, they overlap a lot, and as long as we're talking about magazines and newspapers we might as well touch on it a bit. Sending out a press release or putting together a media kit are both valid marketing activities which are completely within your control.

PR is simply the act of gathering media attention for your business. Ideally, you want this attention to be positive. You're going to try to get mentioned or featured in a magazine or newspaper. Create blogs which again, position you as an expert in your field.

Almost any business can send out a press release when they do something newsworthy. Some businesses may have to get a bit creative to achieve newsworthy things but in general the launch of a new product, a gift to charity, sponsoring a local event, sponsoring a local athlete or competing in some sort of competition all warrant a press release.

Press releases are not the heart and soul of PR, however. You can also perform some basic outreach. For example, if you search the hashtag #journorequest on Twitter, you can watch for reporters who are writing specific stories that are relevant to your business.

Get in touch and explain why you're an expert and how you can contribute to their story. Finding experts is often the hardest part of a reporter's job and many will be more than happy to feature you or your business if you can provide them with helpful information. The interview may not be *about* your business per se, but you'll still get a mention and perhaps a mention of your web address too. Some people will be curious enough to follow that information back to its source so that they can learn what you're all about.

Finally, you should look at any bloggers in your industry so you can reach out to them. For example, you can offer them a free product sample in exchange for a review. If your product or service is featured in a well-known publication then you can use that and say 'As seen in' to give credibility to your marketing materials. Many of these techniques work for television and radio as well, though of course it's much harder to catch the attention of people who are in charge of these channels.

Radio

Commuters are in their cars every day, sometimes for long periods of time, and many of them listen to the radio. This makes radio a good advertising channel for many businesses. Most adverts are only 30 seconds or a minute long, but you can say a lot in that time.

Most radio stations will record your ads for you, so you don't have to worry about hiring professional voice-overs or putting together something in a professional studio. You just give the station your copy and let them do it for you. You need to make sure you use a relevant person for your ad. Think back to your customer avatar, who are they, male or female, how old are they?

The station can run your ad over and over again. You will need to choose how much you're willing to invest and specify at what times of day you would like the ad to go out.

#Quick Tip:

If you use radio make sure you repeat your website address as people will remember it easier than a phone number.

Billboards

Billboards are also a useful local tool, especially if you can get a board that's well-placed to reach your target market. They work best if your proposition is something that can be conveyed very quickly, since you *literally* only have a blink of an eye to catch someone's attention.

I recommend keeping the message clear and concise. If you try to get *too* creative people won't remember anything at all. Billboards are surprisingly affordable.

One billboard might cost anything from £300 to £700 a month. We have used them very successfully on behalf of our clients to promote events.

Brochures

Brochures only work if you have some way to get them into the hands of your intended target audience. If you're going to a trade show, for example, you'll want to invest in them so you can hand them out. If you have a physical mailing list to work with then it might be worth sending some out to existing customers. Sometimes you can put a stack of them in various locations if a lot of your customers visit those locations. I tend to think brochures work best if your business has a strong visual element. There's a good reason why holiday rentals use brochures and accountants generally don't.

Business Cards

Business cards are a good investment for just about everyone. You can hand them out at networking events, meetings and sometimes even at parties when the small talk turns to what you do for a living. You can give a stack to family members or friends who express a willingness to hand them out for you.

The most important thing to remember with business cards is to have them with you at all times.

You won't build a business on business cards alone, but they're good to have. They have a way of circulating around and around, helping you out long after you've forgotten about them. They're also relatively cheap to produce.

#Quick Tip:

If you want to be perceived as a 'proper business' you should always supply more than a mobile phone number on your business card, as well as an email address that is linked to a domain name relevant to your business, and you should never use a website to get free business cards.

Networking Events

Attending networking events should be a part of most people's marketing mix. You can often get a lot more done simply by introducing yourself to other people face-to-face. You can hand out business cards and brochures if you have them. You can talk to people about what they do and hear more about how you can help them. Of course, it helps to be selective about the events you attend—make sure the right people are in the room. Networking is a long term strategy to meet people who you can form relationships with, get to know, love and trust them and only then might you do business together.

#Quick Tip:

Have a plan. Before you attend ask for a delegate list and pick a couple of people you would like to speak to. If you seem to hit it off arrange to see them for a coffee at a later date.

If networking does not come easily to you, try acting like you are the host or hostess and look after everyone else in the room. That way you have a role to play and can forget about your own nerves in favour of making everyone else feel comfortable.

Branded Merchandise

Branded merchandise includes t-shirts, magnets pens, and other items with your business information on it. Pens are inexpensive and do end up passing through a lot of different hands, which means they can keep you at top-of-mind.

They can be used when you've already built up some strong branding in other ways, or if you have some specific place where you're going to be handing them out, such as a trade show or networking event. They can also be a novel way of introducing your company to somebody new.

#Quick Tip:

Research shows that 76% of people remember the names on the promotional items on their desk, with a subsequent 52% of people purchasing from those companies.

Signage

If you run your business in a physical location then you're going to need signs. You'll need a sign out on the street so people can spot your business and know where to enter it. You will probably need a sign on your building somewhere as well. Signs are a necessary part of your marketing mix.

#Quick Tip:

Make sure your signage fits with the rest of the visual identity of your brand. Consistency is key to creating a strong brand.

Directories

Once upon a time everyone had to be in the Yellow Pages. Now, many businesses find their one-line, free entry is more than enough. Still, some businesses find it profitable to take out display ads, and a well-designed Yellow Pages display ad can still get some results for the right type of business. Often trades such as plumbers and electricians can do quite well in them.

The Yellow Pages, however, is not the only directory out there; smaller local directories and professional association directories, can all bear some fruit. Some of these will be focused on both an interest *and* a location, so while they won't reach as many people as some channels will, they'll still be targeted, which means they may accomplish more with the people who *do* see them. There are online directories as well and the principle is much the same. Use directories if they are relevant to you, and skip them if they are not.

YouTube

YouTube is seen as the go to place for information and many major brands are now utilising this media channel. Creating a series of professional looking, informative and eye-catching videos can create some amazing results for you. You can post these videos in multiple places too, on social media channels, *and* on your website as well as on YouTube.

Your business needs to lend itself to making really good videos. Some do, some don't. 'How to' videos play over the best, or 'what you need to know' videos.

Don't write yourself out of the video making process without stopping to brainstorm, at least a little, whether some aspect of your business would fit this marketing channel.

#Quick Tip:

As Google own YouTube, it can also help with your Google Ranking as they tend to favour affiliates of their own company over independent websites.

Websites

Almost every business needs a website and a blog. As 90% of all consumers now go to the web *first* when they want to buy something, there is no question of not being there. You are not going to ask yourself whether you'll be using this particular marketing channel. You're just going to ask yourself *how* you're going to go about using it.

Web pages are a lot more complex than they first appear. You can't just write it up like a big electronic brochure and leave it. You have to think about getting traffic to the site. Fortunately, if you include your web address on most of your other marketing materials then you're already engaging in the process of driving traffic.

You do, however, need to be aware of 'search engine optimisation', or SEO. There are three types most people will have to consider. The first is on-page SEO. This is the process of adding more and more content to your site (usually through blogging) while using relevant keywords targeted to your specialism and your chosen target market.

The second is off-page SEO, where you're going to go around the web, trying to drop some links back to your website. You can do this by guest blogging (the electronic version of an advertorial), by commenting on other people's blog posts, by participating in forums, and through a host of paid methods, such as banner advertising or pay-per-click (PPC) advertising (see below).

The third is local SEO. Local SEO is the process of ranking your business in local and mobile search results, which are generated by Google, Yahoo and Bing. It also describes the process of generating good reviews for your business. There are lots of little tips and tricks for getting your business into the local search results and if you have a physical business serving a distinct geographic area then you're going to need to, either become a master of these tricks, or hire someone else to accomplish them for you.

Direct Mail

Nothing consistently drives money into a business like direct mail. It's practically money in the bank! It offers you the chance to generate a lot of attention because you get to rise above the 'noise' in people's e-mail inboxes.

Ironically, once upon a time, direct mail was viewed with suspicion. People were inundated by 'junk mail'.

Now, most people receive junk e-mail while their physical mailboxes remain empty. Customers now say that they enjoy getting mail and if you can offer it to them in a focused, targeted way then you will be well on your way to making some sales. Every year, direct mail generates £16 billion in sales. It's affordable, it's compelling and most people enjoy receiving it. Even a simple postcard can generate a lot of responses.

E-mail

In spite of all the inbox 'noise', e-mail is still effective. There are two ways to do it without turning yourself into a spammer:

The first way is to offer up some sort of free whitepaper, e-book or report. You can even offer up a whole host of free content in exchange for permission to e-mail the recipient. You continue sending that content and you keep yourself right at the forefront of your prospect's mind.

The second way is to put together a focused, targeted 'cold e-mail', which will be sent to a specific individual. That individual might have a problem that you know about. Perhaps they are your sort of target customer. If you address it directly to them and tailor that e-mail just for them you might get a response.

This is, however, very time consuming, and generally isn't worth it unless you have already made a warm connection (say, at a networking event). You might also do this if you are selling a truly high-value B2B item.

Social Media

Using social media can be one of the fastest and most efficient ways to instantly respond to your customer's unique needs and enquiries. Unlike any other form of customer response and feedback, replies via social media can be individually tailored and personal, ensuring customer satisfaction all around. It's usually a great idea to have some presence on at least one of the major platforms. Make sure your followers are people who are interested in what you have to say. You will be scored on how much interaction you get involved in, and relevant followers are more likely to engage with you.

So if you used your family and friends to get likes on the page it may be time to disconnect from them.

The trick is choosing the platform. A B2B is probably going to spend more time on LinkedIn, as opposed to Facebook. Carefully consider where your customers are and how they use social media before launching any social media plan.

Twitter

Twitter is a perfect platform for establishing yourself as an expert in your field. It also gives you the opportunity to be current and respond instantaneously. For best effect you need to post between six and eight times per day.

Facebook

You need to post about three to four times a day to become credible on Facebook. Using images will add interest and generally help your page look like an interesting place to be.

#Quick Tip:

There are several websites and types of software that will rate your actions on social media sites. These websites can help you monitor what your followers are interested in, as well as what you need to do to become more effective online.

Instagram

Instagram can be used to best effect for businesses that have a very visual message to put out. I have seen it work very well for a company who sell BMX bikes and their loyal followers are keen to receive the notifications and add their own images to the feed.

Banner Ads/PPC Ads

It's easy to waste a lot of money on both of these channels. These are both clickable ad types that will be featured somewhere on the internet. PPC ads (that is, pay-per-click) are usually small, classified type text ads that appear on a search engine results page. Banner ads can appear anywhere but they usually appear on websites. You'll want to carefully choose websites where you *know* your target audience can be found if you're going to use this media.

If you are using Facebook for PPC it is very easy to be extremely specific about whom you want to speak to. You also set the budget so you can start small, test and measure, and then scale the activity up once you know all the elements of the campaign are working.

E-mail Signatures

Don't underestimate the usefulness of this tool. It is a perfect opportunity to make sure people can access you quickly and conveniently. I find it very frustrating when I get emails from people that don't include their phone numbers. The other unforgivable thing in my mind is a web address that isn't a live link to the website.

SMS Text Campaigns

SMS text campaigns can be very effective for some businesses such as shops, coffee shops and restaurants. It usually needs to work side by side with some other form of advertising, since you'll be asking customers to text a certain word to a certain number, usually in exchange for a free food item, a hefty discount or some other reward.

When they do this, they're opting in to a programme that will allow you to send them texts. You would then contact them when you have an upcoming sale, event or other special piece of information to share. Obviously you don't want to abuse the privilege since customers can opt out as easily as they opted in. If you keep the deals exclusive and compelling, however, this is a great way to bring customers back again and again. Text message campaigns have around a 99% open rate, which means people are reading them.

Affiliate Marketing

You can use affiliate marketing any time you sell products online. This involves offering a commission to other marketers, who will promote your product on their own websites and to their own e-mail lists. Since ten marketers can reach many more people than one marketer ever could this is an incredibly effective way to work.

Affiliate marketing is also more useful when your products are very unique and highly branded.

It's hard to market products that anyone can buy at the supermarket, for example. Usually it's a good idea to have a loyal following of your own, since most good affiliates come from your existing customer base.

Joint Ventures

This is when you work with someone else who has the same customer base as you. The best example I ever heard of was when a clothes shop bought a big batch of silk kimonos and they asked a hair and beauty salon in the same geographic location, which had the same age profile of customers, to give their customers a letter saying,

"Thank you so much for your custom. As a token of our appreciation I have bought you a free gift which you can collect from such and such a boutique. Your present is wrapped and waiting for you all you need to do is show them this letter when you arrive."

The take up rate was phenomenal and the return on investment was staggering. I am sure there are people out there who can help spread the word on your behalf.

#Quick Tip:

Spend time building a relationship with a joint venture partner and remember it has to be a win-win for both of you.

Television Advertisements

Most start-ups won't have the money to launch a television commercial campaign. However, you won't be a start-up forever, so it's still worth noting that television might be a viable option in the future.

You can also think beyond commercials. Getting a unique product featured on the Shopping Channel, for example, might well yield some sterling results while increasing your overall exposure.

You could also look to get product placement by getting presenters to use or wear your products. Some programmes also review products.

Seminars and Events

Getting people into a big room for a fun party, an informative seminar, or some other sort of special event can be highly effective. At the end of the event you can book appointments, sell books, or sell products as appropriate.

Obviously you'll need a place to hold the event, and marketing the event can be every bit as intensive as marketing your products and services. But if you pull them off correctly, events generate a lot of buzz. Initially you might just choose four to six of these channels to really focus on and work with.

After all, it's better to offer focused, consistent effort in a few channels than to have scattered, inconsistent efforts in every single channel you can think of. Once you've selected your channels you will need to make a plan for delivering that focused consistent effort.

Once you have those working well, start to introduce new channels working your way up to at least ten.

#Quick Tip:

Always start small, select 10 people to target, measure the response, adjust in the light of take up and feedback. Only scale it up once you know it is working.

Develop and launch a plan

Every successful business is successful in part because it takes the time to create a vision and a plan.

There's no set formula for creating a marketing plan. There are templates online you can model things on, but this isn't something you're going to be showing to anybody other than your own employees, if you have them. So you can write it in Word, you can scrawl it in a spiral notebook or you can print out the whole thing and put it in a ring binder. It can be one page, or it can be 50 pages.

It doesn't matter, as long as you've written it down and committed to it. In fact, the 'business notebook' that I asked you to start contains the very beginnings of a marketing plan and so it might be convenient to just continue using it to develop a more robust plan.

A marketing plan is simply a place where you capture your top-level thinking on which marketing activities you're going to engage in, where you're going to engage in them, and how often you're going to engage in them. You can think of it as a sort of formal 'to-do' list that you're going to follow as you work to build your business.

Having this to-do list makes it far easier to spend your time and money. You begin launching pre-focused campaigns instead of spending time and money on whatever seems good to you at the time. You can also use this plan to pass tasks on to your employees (if you have them); you can even include who is meant for what task as you write your plan.

If you choose to work with a marketing agency they can make suggestions to help you clarify and tighten up your plan, using their experience to help you make it as effective as possible. They would then typically execute the plan so you don't have to—something you might well want them to do by the time you're done writing out every task this plan will demand of you.

A marketing plan should cover at least one year of business. You'll develop a new marketing plan for your second year, and your third year, and so forth. If that feels too daunting a task then start to plan a quarter at a time.

Your plan should include the following items:

- Your core message—the pitch/summary you've already written.
- Your very successful competitor's marketing activity. This is a useful way to guide your own channel and activity selection. Learn from the best; they will have spent a lot of money to find out what works best.

- The channels you intend to target.
- Your editorial calendar and task list for engaging with those channels: what messages will you release, and when.
- Who will be responsible for each of these tasks.
- Your marketing budget.
- Your goals. What would make this marketing plan a success? Going from zero customers to 1 million customers in one year may not make much sense. Going from zero customers to 600 customers in one year might be far more realistic. It is a well known fact that people over estimate what they can do in one year but under estimate what they can achieve in three years.
- Any tests you wish to run, or times when you're going to evaluate marketing results.

You can organise this information in any way that works for you. Just make it clear, easy to read, and easy to follow.

Your marketing plan does demand a budget. If your budget is *zero* then you're going to have to pay for everything in time. **You should plan to put at least 10% of your business revenue back into marketing every month.** This will help you grow your business and will help ensure that you receive a steady stream of clients. You will then have to decide where and how to spend that budget.

Some marketing methods are free—like social media. What you need to do though is develop the mentality that sees marketing spend as an investment; after all, if I gave you a £10 note for every £5 you spent I bet you would be happy to keep spending the £5.

Creating and allocating your budget right now can be very helpful when a slick salesman comes along, suggesting that you spend hundreds of pounds on a new banner ad campaign, or that you should take out a full page ad in the Yellow Pages.

If you didn't have this plan and if you hadn't already done this top level thinking about which channels you were going to use and why then you might be tempted to panic and buy these things because you feel you *need* them. How disappointing, if that impulse buy campaign flops!

While it's not always possible to figure out where *all* of your leads come from, it is a good idea to give yourself your best chance by making sure your money is only going to those places and activities that target the customers you are trying to reach and measuring the effectiveness of the activity.

In order to have the best content you can, as effortlessly as you can, for all the channels you are using I would advise you to develop a content calendar.

This isn't as daunting as it sounds. You're going to start by creating a calendar for each month and on it will be all the channels you are using. So if you're using a blog, social media , direct mail, e-mail marketing and networking events, then you'll need to have them all recorded on the calendar. You'll need to work out the frequency for each channel i.e. a blog post once a week, an e-mail campaign once a month and a Twitter update 7 times a day. The frequency depends on the medium.

Having decided on a frequency you can decide what you'll write about. Blog post topics, Twitter tips, the sale you're having in December... all of it needs to go onto your content calendar. That way you don't have to waste a lot of time trying to decide what you need to write about or put out. You can just get on with the business of creating the content, or having that content created for you.

You may wonder how you can possibly anticipate what you might post or use. After all, many things will happen during the course of your day-to-day business that you might wish to post on your blog, or social media accounts. You might decide to run a special offer to generate some quick sales.

On the other hand, if you *know* you're launching a product in June then April and May should be full of marketing content which leads straight up to that launch.

That needs to be in your calendar, because otherwise June will roll around and you'll find that you've put out a bunch of generic collateral instead of what you really *needed* to put out at that time.

Once you have your entire plan written out on paper, it's time to go back through and evaluate it. Have you really allocated enough money to your budget to do everything that's on your plan?

Have you targeted enough channels to give yourself a good chance of reaching all of the customers you need and want to reach? Have you targeted the *right* channels? If you feel like there's something not quite right or missing, re-evaluate and look for other opportunities. Continue to work with your plan until you feel as though you've developed a truly solid, effective way to capture as much business as possible.

Happy with your plan? It's time to launch! Launching your plan is a matter of taking things one day at a time and offering the persistent, focused effort that you will require to get each of your tasks completed.

If you are doing your own marketing then you should probably plan on devoting at least 20% of your workday to completing your marketing tasks.

Even media buying (that is, purchasing advertising space) takes time and effort. Thus, if you are working an 8 hour day you should assume that your marketing (or working on the business) should probably take up at least 1.6 hours of that day—or an hour and a half, just to make things easy.
If you're taking less time than that then you might want to go ahead and add more to your plan, as it could be an indicator that you haven't targeted enough channels or activities to really make a big difference.

Consistency is absolutely the key to a good outcome. You can't go crazy on your marketing all at once for three weeks, abandon it for six, come back to it in a lacklustre way one week later, and then ignore it for six more. It won't work. You'll never make enough of an impression to really get your message out there. You'll go through 'feast or famine' cycles which will stress you out and burn you out. You'll put your business at risk.

You must complete every task in your plan, or have it completed for you. You must do so even when it gets busy. Otherwise, you won't be very busy for very long.

Obviously some of the tasks on your plan will only need to be completed once. If you're running a newspaper ad then you can just design the ad once, buy the space, and pay for it for any number of months until you decide to test an alternative ad. Other tasks will happen every single day or every single week.

Updating your blog is a never-ending affair, for example, and social media is near-constant as well, especially since you have to take the time to actually talk to people instead of simply pushing out content with some kind of scheduling tool. Having said that it is worth identifying what content can be used time and time again as it is; what is known as evergreen content. It doesn't have any time sensitive material in it.

I recommend breaking each task down into the smallest possible unit so that you don't become overwhelmed. For example, in order to put together a direct mail campaign you have to choose your post codes or develop your mailing list in some way. That's one task. Then you actually have to write the letter.

That's another task. Then you have to print the letters and send them. A third task. You aren't going to try to do all three of those tasks in one day. Any one of them could take up all 1.6 hours of marketing time. Breaking down these tasks will allow you to maximise your time and make the most of it.

You need to consistently work on your business to see the results you need in a consistent way. You might get a customer or two here and there, enough to stay afloat, but you won't see a flood of new customers just because you started posting on your blog and running some ads this week.

You have to be prepared to wait a few weeks for your marketing efforts to start paying off. As you know you'll be getting busy anyway, you might as well spend the extra time working ahead on your marketing plan, so you will be more prepared when things get really busy.

Of course, your time may also be better spent making products, performing sales calls, or engaging in other activities, depending on where you decided to allocate your personal resources. The principle is the same if you're using a marketing agency. Don't just pay them for two months, and then decide they aren't giving you the results you want fast enough. Be in there for the long haul and give your marketing agency some time to work.

Some business owners get frustrated too fast, stopping and starting marketing campaigns before they really have time to accomplish anything. They panic and get tired of paying the overhead, that's because they don't have a marketing investment mentality.

It's a bad idea, because if you *don't* give the plan time to work you've spent all that time and all that money to accomplish nothing at all. Marketing requires momentum. If you stop the machine in its tracks it has to start up all over again before you can accomplish anything at all. Never stop the machine. Once you have your plan, *let it roll.*

That's not to say that you shouldn't improve your plan while it's in action. Obviously we want your marketing to be the best it possibly can be. That's why we've built tests into your plan, and why you start with just ten people till you get it right. You're just not going to bring the entire marketing plan to a *screeching halt* as a result of those tests. Instead, you're going to use them to refine and improve what you're already doing.

Roll it out, monitor it, test it, and then *roll it out again.*

Test it, monitor it and roll it out again

It's very easy to waste time and money on marketing, even when you don't have a plan. That is because when you are a start-up most of your marketing is happening as a result of educated guesses that you are making.

That's not to say your guesses are *bad*. If you sell mail-order pet supplies then your choice to advertise in a magazine catering to pet owners is probably a good one. There's a good chance that the campaign will be very successful.

But you still need to monitor the strength of the campaign so you *know* how successful it is. That way, when you create your Year 2 marketing plan, you'll know exactly how much business it brought in for you. You can make decisions about whether to discontinue the use of that channel, expand upon it, or leave it just as it is.

You also need to test and monitor because getting the message right takes trial and error.

The placement of a single word or the choice of a single phrase can make big differences in the number of sales that you make.

I've seen dramatic changes happen simply because we changed one word in a headline, or used different phrasing on the call to action.

You're dealing with psychology here, and you never have anything more than best practices to fall back on. There's no scientific way of being *absolutely sure* that a piece of writing, or a video, or a radio ad will produce 'X' results until you see that work in action.

That's why you must test every single thing that you do. A piece may work *well*, but it could also work *better*. That little-bitty increase could translate into a huge revenue increase for your business.

This is where many business owners simply drop the ball. They throw their marketing out there without ever analysing what works and what doesn't. Some assume that since they're starting to get business, or have clients now, everything is fine. Unfortunately, everything isn't fine.

Their business isn't running at optimum level, and never will run at optimum level, because they simply don't know where to spend their time, attention or money. Should they take out a half page ad next year or stick with their ¼ page ad?
No clue, because they have no idea how many calls the first ad generated.

Is their website getting enough traffic from their organic efforts, or might it be a good idea to place some banner ads in order to increase visitors? The business owner who doesn't test and monitor simply has no idea.

What are you looking for with all this testing and monitoring? Let's take a moment to go over some terms. There are three metrics that really matter.

The first is **impressions**. That is the number of people who are seeing your ad. You won't always know for sure how many impressions you get. When you advertise online this data is easy to track. If you advertise in a newspaper or magazine you'll really only have the circulation figures which are listed in their media kit.

You can generally assume that all of the subscribers did see your ad, so when you're dealing with print, impressions are an advance decision rather than something you monitor.

When you're looking at your website, however, this will be the number of monthly, daily or weekly visitors that your website receives, stats that Google Analytics will typically track for you.

When you buy banner ads or PPC ads the provider will generally provide these figures; sometimes you'll pay for the number of impressions you receive.

The second metric is **response.** This measures the number of people who took some form of action in response to your advertisement. If you've run a banner ad you'd be measuring the number of people who clicked on your ad. On your website, you might choose to measure how many people downloaded your free giveaway and signed up for your e-mail list. In the e-mail list, you might measure how many people clicked on a link you sent them. Response moves customers just a little closer to buying.

The third big metric is **conversion.** These are the people who actually bought products and services as a result of your marketing efforts. Obviously you don't make any money if you don't convert people.

All together, the three metrics make one big funnel. Impressions create *suspects*, people who *may* be interested.

Some of those suspects respond, and become *prospects*, people who have indeed demonstrated some sort of interest. Prospects become *clients* or *customers* when they convert. Like any funnel, there will always be more action in the top. If you get 10,000 suspects you might get 1,000 prospects, which leads to 100 clients.

If you don't keep marketing and don't keep making a consistent effort, then you never pour more people into the top of that funnel, which means business eventually dries up.

These metrics are the ones which tell you whether or not your marketing campaign is *really* working. After all, the purpose of any marketing campaign is to generate leads which ultimately turn into sales. If you're not getting any leads and you're not making any sales then your campaign isn't helping you. As you watch these analytics you're going to pay attention to the amount of time or money that you've spent vs. the leads that you've received. If you spent £500 to run an ad and got just 3 customers out of that ad you might well decide to drop that marketing channel in the future. The return on investment just wasn't enough to justify continuing unless those 3 customers each spent £2,000 or so. If each customer spent £22.99 then that ad has cost you money.

Don't forget to factor your *time* as you make these decisions. Your time is absolutely worth money. If you could have made more by doing people's taxes than you made writing all those blog posts then it is time to outsource the blog posts. If it takes you 4 hours a day to launch marketing campaigns, leaving you just 4 hours a day to do tax returns, then you're not really getting a good return on the investment simply because your earning potential is limited by your available time and you've lost most of that time attempting to do your own marketing. Testing and analysing what you are doing will help you continue to make decisions about whether or not you are really the best person to take on the marketing role.

Now these are not the only metrics you can measure. Individual marketing channels might come with other metrics that you'll want to watch. Website analytics include 'bounce rates', for example, which tell you how long a prospect was on your website before moving on to other things. That's certainly a metric you would want to watch, because it tells you how interesting and compelling your site is. It also tells you how much of your traffic is actually targeted, and how much is landing there by mistake.

On social media, you would want to watch 'engagement'. That metric tells you how many likes, comments or retweets you get when you post new content.

Likes and retweets don't directly translate into any kind of sales or money but they *do* tell you whether or not people are actually paying attention to your brand. If people are paying attention then they are likely to buy at some point—or buy again, if they are already customers.

Your marketing plan should include your goals and success benchmarks for *each channel* in addition to those 'big 3' marketing metrics.

If you choose to be on Twitter then you might make growing your following by 50 people every month a benchmark goal, so that you can walk away with roughly 600 followers at the end of your first year.

So when you do your quarterly review, you can ask yourself if those numbers are on target. If you're falling short, you'll know that you need to do more: adjust your content, perhaps, or follow more targeted accounts. If you're exceeding your goals then you know that you're handling Twitter correctly and you can turn your attention to optimising other campaigns and maybe even setting new goals.

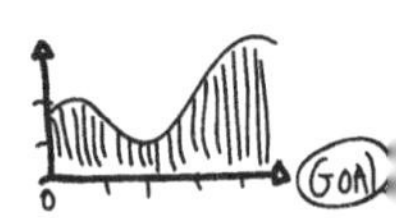

* Watching analytics is not enough if you don't have some strategy in place that will help you improve them. This is where split testing comes in. Split testing is a method for testing the effectiveness of your advertisements.

Proven Strategies for Success

It involves launching one ad, an 'A' ad, and then launching another one, a 'B' ad, that is similar but not the same. You would then measure response. In order to do this, you need some way of telling which responses came from which ad.

In a print or radio ad you'd generally do this by setting up a special phone number for each ad. On your e-mail list you might just segment your list right in half, sending one half the A ad and one half the B ad.

On your website there are actually programs that will show your visitors different versions of the site, and will measure their response. You would run this test for about 30 days and watch what happens.

One of the two ads is going to perform better. Once you've ascertained which one of them does so, you can scrap the underperforming ad and run the successful one into the future.

Of course, it's not a bad idea to *keep* testing. Your third version might perform *even better*. You can also build landing pages to see which channel is driving traffic by creating one for each channel, i.e. Twitter, Facebook, LinkedIn, etc.

This is why you wrote testing periods into your marketing plan. If you already know that you're going to launch tests once every quarter then you will make the room and the time to write those alternative ads. You can watch how these ads perform against each other and make incremental improvements.

Sometimes the very first ad you put together will be the winner, every time. Sometimes the sixth ad you put together will generate your best response. In either case, you're leaving money on the table if you don't take the time to find out which ad is the best ad. It's as simple as that.

Now you're armed with a lot of information. You can decide to drop some marketing channels while spending or focusing more on others.

You can figure out how to duplicate truly successful campaigns so that you continue to enjoy a fantastic response. Testing and analysing your campaigns gives you everything you need to turn your marketing roll-out into a well-oiled machine, something which starts generating reliable revenue for your business.

In time, you should understand how to spend £1 on marketing in order to make £100 in sales (as an example).

People refer to marketing as 'overheads,' and it can be, if you don't test. If you test, analyse, and then roll out a new, improved version of your campaigns on a regular basis it becomes an 'investment', and that's right where you are going to want it to be. It's time consuming, but it's definitely worth it, and it is absolutely what separates successful businesses from unsuccessful businesses. You now begin to understand why the old saying, "I know only half my advertising works, but I don't know which half", is lunacy.

Why would you keep spending money on the half that doesn't work, especially when you've got methods to determine which half does?

Proven Strategies for Success

Chapter Four

Purple!

Staying on track

Pursing personal growth

Getting support

Part 4: Purple!

Why do we love the colour purple so much? It's simple! Purple impacts the body, mind and spirit in a very positive way and, here at WAM, we believe in being *very* positive indeed! In fact, we believe that your ability to be as positive as possible actively impacts the success or failure of both your marketing plan *and* your business.

If your body, mind and spirit are not in alignment with your goals, then you're going to falter. You won't have the internal stamina to pursue your marketing goals. Instead, you'll get overwhelmed or you'll procrastinate. You might get frustrated or impatient when it's too early to do so. You might find it impossible to get all of your ideas down on paper because they're flying around in your head along with your fears and frustrations. You will want to avoid 'putting yourself out there' because you'll fear the response and you'll end up doing what a lot of people do, which is hope that offering a service or building a product are going to be enough to just magically bring people to your door.

So, while this section isn't going to teach you more about calculating marketing metrics or engage you in the process of building or discovering your brand, it's still one of the most important sections of the book.

Proven Strategies for Success

I'm going to show you how to programme your mind into a tool which supports and enhances your ability to succeed. I will teach you how to stay on track, so that your marketing is actually fun and interesting to you. The last thing I want is for your marketing to feel like an enormous chore. Instead, you should see your marketing efforts as the petrol which fuels your business.

This is important because your potential and actual clients will be able to pick up on the way that you feel about your business and the way that you feel about marketing your business. You'll want your marketing messages to be infused with an enthusiastic, passionate and positive energy so that it acts like a magnet, attracting customers straight to you.

Your mind set will make a business even if you outsource your marketing. It will make the difference between viewing your marketing company as a *partner* and viewing them as an annoying, stressful expense. If your feelings about marketing are negative, then sooner or later you're going to decide that paying for marketing is a low-priority activity. You'll end up pulling the plug on campaigns that might have worked for you before they get a chance to start offering results, and you'll be right back where you started, and you can't afford that!

Staying on track

Marketing is often the first thing to fall by the wayside when money is tight or when business gets busy. There are several reasons for this.

The first is that most business owners just honestly do not enjoy, or see the value in, marketing. It is not what they are good at, and it is not what they'd rather be doing. As discussed, most business owners would rather be following their passion. Some business owners discover a hidden talent for marketing, or find they enjoy it a great deal, but that's not always the case.

In my own particular case I don't enjoy working on finance, whether that is raising invoices, paying suppliers or chasing payment. For that reason, that part of my business has been done by other people right from the start. I would rather keep my passion for what I am good at, which is working with businesses to help them grow.

The second reason is that marketing doesn't give anyone instant gratification. When you make a sales call you might sign a contract where money changes hands right away. You deliver your product or your service and you get the reward.

The action-to-reward cycle is *not* fast when you're dealing with marketing. You could put out an ad and wait two or three weeks before you actually hear a response from that ad.

It could take you several months to start getting significant traffic to your website. You may get customers—and they may not be able to tell you exactly where they heard about you. We live in an instant gratification culture to begin with, so it's really little wonder that many people find this longer action-to-reward cycle so very frustrating.

You already know that letting your marketing fall to the bottom of your priority list is a good way to derail your chances of achieving long-term business success. Thus, it's important to have some strategies that will help you stay on track. Here are several that you can use.

Identify your slow times

As we've mentioned before, you'll need to spend about 20% of your work time on your marketing if you choose to do it yourself. In a 40 hour work week you'll want to commit to about 7.5 hours. I am aware that few business owners work less than 60 hours a week, but we're going to use 40 because I want to give you realistic, workable figures to run with.

7.5 hours is reasonable but it can get away from you very quickly. When you've got a project that has to be completed right away, or a print deadline to meet, marketing is the last thing on your mind. When are you going to get it all done?

It's best to identify your slow periods. That may be an entire day (you may, for example, never have much business on Tuesdays) or it may be a certain *time* of day, such as the mornings before people start calling, coming in, or e-mailing you.

Once you have this information, you can use it to create a routine. You can simply block it into your schedule. Tuesday will be your marketing day and you're not going to use it for anything else: not sales, not service, nor operational issues.

Then, when you sit down to use this 7.5 hours you're going to be productive as never before. You're going to sit down with your marketing plan and you're going to break the day's work into a series of focused to-dos which are actionable, immediate, and taken down to their smallest possible tasks.

By the time you're finished you should feel very accomplished indeed, and confident that you can do it all over again next week. In time, this work should become second nature to you, just another necessary part of your business work day.

Focus on what you can control

You can't *make* people respond to your marketing. You want to know what the response is, of course, and you want to improve it. But it's not a good idea to *focus* on that response. Instead, you want to focus on what *you* can do to build your business.

You cannot control the number of people who respond to your ads, but you can control how good the ads are and make sure they are in the best place to be seen by your target market.

You can't control how long it takes for your website to start gaining traffic, but you can control how often you post to your website and whether you put the consistent effort into building it up, to give it the time that it requires to gain that momentum.

You can't control the number of people who sign up for your e-mail list, but you can make sure that your offer is the very best offer it possibly can be.

You can't control the number of retweets you receive, but you can control what you post and you can learn about what kinds of posts gain the most retweets in general.

For example, you can commit to using more pictures after learning that visuals get more likes and retweets than any other type of content.

You can control testing and analysing your results, too. You can control your ability to learn more about how to do each of these tasks a little better tomorrow than you're doing them today. You can launch better versions of the work you're doing right now so that your marketing grows stronger with every passing day.

In other words, you can control taking the right actions in the right way, each and every day, so you get a response that you can be pleased with in time. You will find that if you focus on doing what you can that the results will tend to follow. You may even be pleasantly surprised by the way those results pan out. That's because you've shifted your focus to doing enough of the right things in the right way.

Before you understood how important this was, you might not have done things consistently and therefore wouldn't have had as a good a result.

Seek momentum

Marketing is all about building *momentum.* You have to put yourself out there consistently. What you do this week builds on what you did last week, and both efforts are greater for what you did the week before. That's why you don't want to stop once you've got started. You want to keep going and going so that people get a chance to seamlessly interact with your brand on a regular basis.

If you stop this momentum at any point you'll have to begin at the beginning all over again. That is a good way to waste time, money and effort.

Once you have gained momentum you start to get traction and then once that happens you are on a roll. It's a bit like riding a bike it takes more effort to get your speed up but once it is you don't have to pedal as hard. If you stop though, you'll have to start the process all over again.

Keep learning

Every marketing method is different. Each of the channels I've shared with you could have whole books written about that single channel alone. Indeed, many of those books *have* been written!

If you want to improve your marketing, you're going to have to commit to learning more about each channel you intend to use. Don't let "I don't know how" stop you.

Now, at first, it's enough to just jump in there and *do something*. Many business owners don't even get that far. You want to start blogging or tweeting or putting out videos, even if it feels awkward and even if the finished product doesn't look and feel as nice as you might like at first. Right at the beginning it's just important to do it, so long as whatever you are doing is 100% consistent with your brand.

Later, however, you'll want to be as effective as possible. You'll want to know what others have done to get better results. You'll want to know how to duplicate those results for yourself and every piece of information you acquire gives you more of an opportunity to do better. Yesterday it was enough to put out your first video. Today, you want to learn about video lighting so that tomorrow's video looks even better.

This is so important that I recommend setting aside at least a small portion of your marketing time to learning more about marketing; 30 minutes of reading or watching tutorials could pay great dividends later.

The information is always out there, so don't let confusion or a lack of knowledge stop you or scare you. We live in the Information Age and everything you need to know is literally at your fingertips and often available for free.

Stop, take a deep breath, and go find the information that you need.

Obviously at some point there may be a cost-benefit analysis where you decide that learning this new skill isn't the best use of your time. But if you really feel strongly about pursuing your own marketing it's one of the best ways to become successful at it.

'Nothing' is the worst thing you can do

Many business owners let the 'perfect' become the enemy of 'the good'. But you don't have to be perfect. You just have to get out there. Remember, this is just about communicating with other people and telling them about something which might serve them or help them. You've been communicating all your life. All of the channels that we've talked about are just tools to help you *talk*.

Don't get so caught up in the idea that you might be 'doing it wrong' that you never do anything at all.

Take a 'ready, [illegible] fire, aim' approach.

Purple!

Roll out your marketing plan, then analyse it, test it, refine it, and roll it out again. That's all part of the process. In one year your marketing plan will be absolutely amazing. In your first three months it's perfectly normal to feel as though you are simply fumbling along day after day.

There is, after all, a bit of a numbers game at work. If you reach 100 people badly one person may still respond. That's one more customer than you would have had if you had done nothing at all!

Now you just have to figure out how to reach 100 more people just a little better, so that three people respond next time, instead of just one. This is the game that professional marketers play every single day.

If you take the 'ready, aim, fire' approach you're likely to stay stuck in 'aim' mode for too long. You won't do anything, because you'll be so busy trying to get it just right that you never launch what you've got. Just give it your best shot right now.

See your business as one of your clients

Have you ever heard that old adage about saving money which says that you should "pay yourself first"? In a sense, you can apply this adage to marketing your business, too.

You should treat your business like one of your clients. It's important to satisfy your paying clients. You want to give your customers the products or services they've asked for. That's of course, how you stay in business.

However, your business needs attention too. Marketing is one way that you service your business. You should schedule time to work for your business just like you schedule time to work for your clients and customers. That means that you're giving those marketing tasks priority on your to-do list. You're assigning yourself marketing deadlines that are just as important as the project deadlines, which you are giving out to your clients, and you're taking them just as seriously.

At WAM we have 'WOW time' which we put in our calendars, and this means 'Working on WAM'. It is a discipline to do it and not get distracted but the rewards are worth it.

Purple!

If you find that you just don't have enough hours in your day to give your marketing this much priority then you need to invest money into allowing someone else to make it *their* task priority. Your business is in one of two predicaments: you either have more time than money, or more money than time. Decide which predicament you are in, and act accordingly.

Make the connection

Nothing is more motivating than drawing a direct link between your marketing efforts and the money those efforts make for you. That's another great reason why you should be observing where most of your business is coming from. It helps you build that link. It helps show you how and where your hard work is paying off the most.

You may not have this data yet, and that's okay. Every time you engage in marketing activities just say, "This is going to make money for me." Everything you do builds a complete picture of your business in the minds of your customers.

In fact, this is true even if the marketing collateral didn't seem to send a single direct customer your way. You might ask, "How did you hear about us?" Customers might answer, "Google". Does that mean you wasted all that time you poured into blogging?

Not necessarily. If you showed up in the Google searches your marketing activity got you there.

Furthermore, the radio ad the customer heard last week put the idea of searching for you into their head in the first place. Following your marketing plan makes money for your business, there's no doubt about it. Some channels and activities will be more profitable than others but even a campaign which totally flops reaches *someone*. And it teaches you more about your business, your brand, and your marketing strategy, too. There really is no such thing as a complete waste of marketing time or marketing money so long as you are continuing to build that all-important momentum.

Make sure you are actually using your plan

Some people write marketing plans—and then never look at them again. That's a good way to fail. You need to use the plan you've worked so hard to build. Don't try to rely on your memory either. That's a good way to stray and to get off track.

Your plan is an excellent road map for everything you need to do. Make sure that you are following it to the letter. Check those items off of the to-do list and feel proud of what you've accomplished.

Take care of yourself

This tip doesn't necessarily relate to marketing alone. It relates to every part of doing business. You're working hard. You're trying to juggle a lot of tasks and a host of different roles.

You're overcoming new challenges and learning how to do new things every single day. Don't forget to take some time to breathe. Do something nice for yourself or take a break. It's hard to get other people excited about your business, your vision, and your mission when you would rather roll over and go back to sleep yourself. You need to have that passion inside of you so that you can share it with others. Keeping your energy levels high is the best way to ensure that your passion levels remain good and strong.

By the way, don't forget to eat right, sleep and exercise. Your body impacts your mind and if your body isn't in good shape you'll find it much harder to conquer the challenges in front of you.

Look back to your 'why'

Are you having trouble getting everything done?
If so, then it's time to look back to your 'WHY'.
Why are you in business in the first place?
What was important enough for you to take this risk?

It's often a lot easier to go to work for someone else than it is to be in business for yourself. You must have had a strong, powerful why to catapult you into business.

There must have been a very big desire burning inside of you. Reconnect with that desire when you start to lose your motivation. Think about the rewards you hope to attain. Think about the rewards you already *have* attained. If you're doing what you love, remind yourself why you love it.

If you wanted more time with your family go spend some of that time with them so that you can recharge your batteries and get back out there. There is a reason why I began by asking you about your 'why,' and this was one of those reasons. Your 'why' is capable of pushing you forward, even when the going gets tough. In business, the going can get very, very tough indeed. Reconnecting with your why will remind you that this is all worth it!

Pursuing personal growth

If you want to succeed you need to get what we at WAM call the 'money making mentality.' You actually have to train your mind to support your business goals. Otherwise, your mind will defeat you every time.

You want something: a successful business and you might think that your willpower is all you need to make it happen.

If you know what to do you just have to get out there and do it. Unfortunately, if your willpower conflicts with your imagination in any way, then you're not going to succeed. Your imagination is going to win.

You're busy pushing, pushing and pushing. You're *willing* yourself to get out there and make sales, or to set up your website, or to do whatever it takes to keep your business afloat. However, your imagination is busy serving up images of failure; images of having to go back and beg for your old job. Of having to tell your spouse that you didn't succeed. You might have visions of financial ruin. Or you might just be afraid of being rejected, laughed at, or called a fraud or a phony.

As a result, your anxieties take over. You start sabotaging yourself in a thousand tiny ways. You write your blog post, but you don't remember to proof read it, and it ends up hurting your brand rather than helping it. You sit down at your computer to work, but you can't find the energy to get the job done, so you end up checking your e-mail for the thousandth time today.

Your fears overcome you, and you push your messages out timidly, if you push them out at all. Your imagination steals all of the strength from you.

Thus, we've got to work to **get your imagination on your side**. That's the only way your entire mind is going to be energised, alert, passionate and ready to succeed. Getting your imagination on your side is what the money mind set is all about.

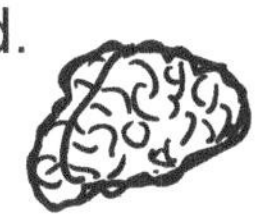

In order to do this, you must programme your subconscious mind to work with you. Your imagination flows out of your subconscious and that's what makes it so insidious. You might not even be *aware* of the dozens of ways that you are hurting yourself if you don't take the time to set your subconscious straight. That's because we're generally only aware of what's going on in our conscious minds.

Fortunately, you don't have to know everything that your subconscious is doing in order to programme it to your advantage. However if you can grasp the concept that the subconscious mind does not recognise the difference between the truth and a lie and use that knowledge to your advantage you are on to a sure-fire winner.

The subconscious works between building a series of associations between the events we experience consciously and the feelings we associate with those events.

If someone says something nasty to you at a party and you feel bad your subconscious might start to equate 'going to a party' with 'feeling unhappy.'

Purple!

As a result, you feel anxious at your next party and you don't have very much fun. The association is then strengthened, even if nobody said anything particularly nasty to you at that party. Pretty soon you start avoiding parties altogether. You may even start avoiding people altogether.

Later, you start thinking that you've been alone for an awfully long time and you'd like to improve your social life. So you go out and try to start making friends. That's what your will wants, and so you use your will power to go meet people at a coffee shop.

But your imagination is already busy extrapolating things. It is thinking, "You've just met this cool new person at a coffee shop. If this friendship is allowed to progress, I'll probably get invited to a party. I don't really like parties. I don't do very well at parties. I sure hope this person doesn't invite me to a party."

You go home and later the phone rings. Your new friend leaves a message. You end up being 'too busy' to answer the message. You'll do it later. You aren't really avoiding your new friend so much as you're avoiding that imagined party but the result is the same. You never call back and the new friendship dries up and blows away.

What would have happened if you had started building some positive feelings and associations into your subconscious response *before* you started trying to go after what you wanted to do and accomplish? The outcome probably would have been very different.

To do this, you will select new, positive thoughts. You're going to do this consciously. After all, your conscious mind is the part of your brain that you get to control. As you do this, your subconscious mind will record and store these new, positive associations.

In order to do this, you must first notice the moment that you are having negative feelings. This will alert you to the fact that your subconscious mind has built a negative association. When you don't take that call from your friend your conscious mind may not give you anything other than vague discomfort. You might just think, "I don't really feel like talking to anyone right now."

You probably don't think of that awful moment at the party ten years ago.

However, that avoidance is still a signal that you have some negative associations going on, and it's a signal that you can and should do some conscious reprogramming.

You might simply choose one positive statement like, "I love getting phone calls from my friends!" That one thought may be enough to have you call your friend back there and then.

If not, you'll at least be ready to call in an hour or two, when you've finished doing whatever it was that you were doing in the first place. You can use that thought every time you look at the phone, in fact. Even saying something so positive will generally give you positive feelings to go with them.

What kinds of feelings are you feeling as you draft up your marketing plan? Have you felt bored? Irritated? Frustrated? Overwhelmed? These are all signs that you have some negative associations with growing your business that need to be replaced.

Note that you don't have to go delving into your brain to figure out what, exactly, gave you that negative association. You don't need to figure out that you're having all of this trouble because growing your business reminds you that you might need to speak in public and the thought of public speaking reminds you of when you had to give a speech in your Year 4 classroom and the bullies laughed you off the stage. You simply have to consciously select the thoughts that will serve you better, and do so the moment that you notice that you are experiencing these negative feelings about yourself, your marketing or your business.

What sorts of thoughts might you choose? You might say, "I love introducing myself to customers!" Since marketing is *all about* introducing yourself to customers this positive statement may very well suffice to get your head back in the game.

You can take a moment to close your eyes and experience what it will be like to gain that new customer. Maybe you'll meet in person and shake hands, and you'll have a big grin on your face as you seal the deal. Maybe they'll send £500 straight to your bank account so you can start work on their project or send out that product. Pick an image that makes you feel really happy. Sooner or later it's the happy images, thoughts and associations that will drive your actions, rather than the unhappy ones.

Another way to programme your mind is to watch the way that you talk to yourself about the tasks that you're facing. Sometimes our conscious mind does get in on the negativity action and you can hear it loud and clear. Listen to how you speak and think sometimes. Ask yourself what you are saying about:

- Your business
- Yourself, as a business owner
- Marketing
- Your ability to market your business

Are any of those statements really negative? For example, you might hear yourself saying, "I guess I'm okay at what I do, but there are so many other people out there who are so much better than I am."

What a way to sap your passion and enthusiasm! You've got to turn that around, and quick! So instead you might choose to say: "There are lots of people who need my skills and my approach just as they are right now. I can't wait to meet them!"

You might hear yourself saying, "I can't do it. I'm just no good at marketing." To which you might say, "I can easily follow the tasks in my marketing plan." Or, "I don't *have* to be good at marketing. I just have to be good at running my business and sticking to my plan."

Look at how much more motivating these thoughts and statements are. Choosing these thoughts actively empowers you and gives you more energy to run your business in a successful way. The quality of your life and the success of your business truly are determined by the quality of your thoughts!

You can do this for virtually any negative thought that you experience. This kind of thinking can help you in virtually every area of your life.

As you craft your positive thoughts remember positive statements are most powerful when they're in the present tense. You don't get into an argument with your subconscious about what happened yesterday if you're hyper-focused on what's going on *today*. Yesterday, that party was awful. There's no need to dispute that. But *today* you "love receiving calls from new friends." You have decided it, and it's true.

It will ring true to your subconscious as well. But if you try to say, "I've *always* loved receiving calls from my friends" your subconscious will reject the statement. It can easily access all of the times that you didn't really love receiving those calls, and it will play those times out in your mind.

You can even use the words, "I choose." "I choose to have a vibrant, fun social life." There's nothing the subconscious can say in response to that. It can't say, "Yeah but, remember that time?" You're choosing. Your choice has nothing to do with yesterday. Your choice has everything to do with today.

"I choose to make marketing my business a priority."
"I choose to have fun marketing my business."
"I choose to invest money into my business so I can reap the rewards and benefits."

Purple!

See how powerful all of those statements are? See how they instantly lift your mood? You'll open yourself up to more inspiration. You'll gain clarity and energy to accomplish all of the things which you must accomplish to be a successful business owner. These kinds of statements lift a fog away from your brain immediately and they gain momentum over time, just as your marketing gains momentum over time. Start today and be consistent because the more you use this technique the more you will reap the benefits of the technique.

Watch out for common pitfalls

There are nine very common mental pitfalls that business owners should be watching out for. These pitfalls can undermine your attempts to programme your subconscious to your advantage.

* The first is **'all-or-nothing' thinking**. "This campaign is a total failure if I don't get 500 new customers in six months." Is it? Is it a *total* failure? What if you got 200 new customers? That would still be a pretty good outcome, wouldn't it? It might indicate that your original goal was unrealistic, or it might indicate that there's room for improvement in your strategy. Someone with an all-or-nothing mind set, however, would skip straight to cancelling the entire campaign.

This would be a shame, since the campaign has already proven it can bring in 200 customers every six months. The business owner cheats themselves out of the 200 customers they could have had because life didn't conform to their exact specifications.

The second is **'having to be perfect'**. When you do this it's very hard to launch anything at all. You're too busy trying to 'perfect it'. But you don't have to be perfect! You just have to be genuine as you share your brand with other people. In fact, perfection is impossible. You could sit for months without doing anything at all if perfection is your goal, because you simply are never going to achieve it. Sometimes good enough is good enough. *

The next mistake is succumbing to an **'I don't know how'** narrative. While I don't advocate trying to become a master of every business skill, I do think that there are always going to be times when a business owner will have to tackle thought processes and situations which they've never faced before. Start replacing this one with "I can learn" right away. You might also try, "I can solve any problem that comes my way." Being an entrepreneur is *all about solving problems.* You're actually getting paid to think about solutions and to deliver them. When you are saying, "I don't know how", you're actually stopping your creativity—that portion of your mind you're getting paid to exercise—in its tracks! *

* The next pitfall is a very natural **fear of rejection**. You're putting yourself out there, so naturally you might worry that you're going to get shot down. What if you do this and *nobody* responds?

What if you do it and people accuse you of not being genuine? What if you do it and everyone you know sees you look foolish? These fears crop up for business owners quite often.

Just do it! You'll soon see that most of your fears are unwarranted. People put themselves out there every day, and nothing terrible happens. They even make mistakes while they do it and discover that there's no great black list in the sky that punishes them.

If you just do it great crowds will not surge out to point and laugh at you because something wasn't right, and they won't come out to burn you at the stake, either! As long as we look at what happened and learn from it, all is good. Test your ideas, measure their success and improve on the results.

You can change your thoughts in this way: "People *want* to hear my message because I'm sharing it with those who will be really interested in it!" You can also say, "I talk to the right people in the right way and those people benefit immensely from doing business with me."

Fear of failure may seem warranted given the business statistics I shared with you at the beginning of this book. After all, you know that you're trying to become part of a very elite group: the 5% of business owners who succeeded. *

Here's the problem: this fear is not very productive. If you're doing everything you can do today to give your business its best possible chance at success, then that is all anyone can possibly ask from you. You're reading this book, for example, and if you've made it this far I'm pretty confident that you're ready and willing to put most of the training encompassed in this book right into action.

In the meantime, worrying about failure steals all of your energy away. You *need* that energy to run your business! In this regard, failure becomes a self-fulfilling prophecy if you dwell upon it for too long. You can be *aware* of the possibility of failure without letting the fear of failure take over your life or sap your strength. Instead, say, "I'm doing everything I can today to help ensure my business success."

Remember, too, that some of the richest people on the planet failed multiple times before they succeeded.

Some people fear the little failures as often as they fear the big failures. You might as well take a deep breath, though, and accept they're going to happen.

You can serve clients faithfully for five years without ever missing a deadline only to find you've made mistakes in meeting *two of them*, in the same week. All you can do is pick yourself up and move on, resolving to do better. Some people don't do that however. They let those small failures derail their entire business strategy. The small failures then go on to become one big failure, and the business dies.

You can choose this thought, "I am always learning, and I get better at what I do every single day."

Some people have the opposite problem, however. They have a **fear of success**. Sooner or later you start to realise that success will make a lot of demands on you that you might not necessarily feel ready for. Your business may soon be taking you to places that are bigger than you currently are right now. You might not feel ready for them. You might fear that when you get there, everything will fall apart, or that you'll be exposed as a fraud because you just don't *feel* like a big business owner yet.

The answer to this one is, "I can grow as big as my dream needs me to grow!" Remember, you always have the option to continue learning and to solve problems. You even have the option to make some mistakes.

Success will feel great, and when you get there it will not be because you 'faked' your way there.

Finally there's the belief, **"This just isn't working!"** This belief is born out of frustration. I know you want things to move really fast. I know that when you launched your business you envisioned achieving wild success in a matter of months, or even weeks. Sometimes it takes longer than that. *

Your answer to this is, "I'm focusing on the things I can control." Remember, everything you want will come if you just continue to do the right things in the right way in a consistent fashion. You can't control the when, but you can control the how. Running your business is almost exactly like going for a drive.

Sometimes the roads are smooth and empty. Sometimes there's an enormous traffic jam which forces you to inch forward bit by bit. You can't do anything but continue to push the pedals and turn the wheel in the right direction, confident that if you keep at it you're going to get exactly where you need and want to go.

Make your choice

Notice the role of choice in this process. Ultimately, the success or failure of your business is up to you. You're making a series of **choices** about your outcomes. You're going to choose whether or not to engage in the activities that help you. You're going to choose whether or not to believe in yourself. You're going to choose whether or not you're going to consciously change your thoughts.

Some people look to external circumstances to explain their success or failure.

It's true that external circumstances can have an impact on the story of your business. Yet two people could face the exact same setback while ultimately producing quite dissimilar results.

One business owner loses a big client and reels from the setback so much that they never get another big client again. Eventually they close their doors, because 90% of their income was coming from that specific person or company. They lose their confidence and don't recover.

Down the street, another business owner loses a big client and throws themselves into their marketing to replace that client.

They also decide that they are never giving *that much* of their time and attention to any one person again. Ten years later they have expanded, taken on more employees, and have six times as many clients as they had before.

They both had the same external circumstance but they both chose very different thoughts. Business Owner A thought the loss of that client meant that they were a failure. That they were sunk; that they couldn't possibly find another client in time to make it through the month. In time, they started thinking that it was all the client's fault—or the fault of whatever caused the client to cancel in the first place. "I was in business once", they say later.

"But the economy got really bad and I couldn't keep my doors open." Everyone who hears their story nods their head sympathetically.

Business Owner B allowed the loss of that client to teach them something about their business. They stepped up their efforts. Their thought was, "These things happen sometimes. Let me think how I can do things better next time." They took total responsibility for the fate of their business, even though it would have been easy to blame their former client, the economy, their competitors, or any number of other people or things for their momentary setback.

In fact a lot of people like to play the martyr and blame someone else instead of taking responsibility for themselves. We can even get a lot of sympathy and attention by adopting that way of thinking.

However a successful business owner has no need for sympathy and attention, in that way. A successful business owner is only concerned with what it takes to succeed. That's why successful business owners spend so much time focusing on **personal development.** They know and understand that their own business will only develop and grow in direct correlation to their own personal growth.

If you aren't accustomed to taking personal responsibility then you have to *develop* that aspect of your character. If you aren't used to positive thinking then you have to learn, grow and develop the mental muscles that allow you to catch your negative self-talk, turning it around before it grows destructive.

Your business growth will be stunted until you conquer these ways of thinking. If you want to foster this development it is helpful to give yourself a mental workout. In fact, some of the most successful business owners in the world take the time to do this 'workout' every single day.

Performing a mental workout is easy. Choose some personal development books or audio books. Carve out some time to read them or listen to them during the course of your day. Let them lift you up and fill you with the different possibilities. Let them arm you with dozens of techniques for controlling your thoughts, programming your mind and achieving your best future. I like to do this first thing in the morning because it puts me in the right frame of mind to tackle my entire day.

You should also take the time to study successful business leaders. Many highly successful men and women have written books about their experiences. You can use them to learn what they did in order to succeed. You'll be able to emulate some of their techniques in order to foster your own success. You'll get a sense of how these successful business people view the world and as you absorb more of their worldview into yourself you'll gain an additional understanding of how to carry this wisdom into your own business.

The success formula

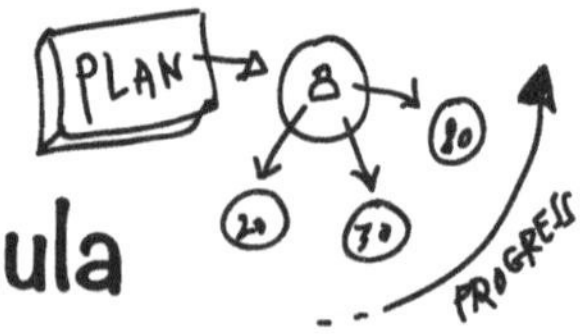

Everything you've been hearing about is part of the 'Success Formula.' This formula teaches you the essential elements of success and successful people. If you look really closely, you'll see that these principles even spell out the word 'successful!'

Substitute negative thoughts for positive ones. Work on this every day. Work on it even when you feel like life is giving you a hard time. In fact, I'd suggest that substituting negative thoughts for positive ones should be something you constantly strive to be aware of.

Use motivational quotes and affirmations. This is a big part of training your brain. It's hard to be negative when you are filling your mind with as much positive self-talk as possible. Sometimes it's hard to generate that from within, so reading or listening to those who have already mastered this formula can provide you with a boost—and a steady diet of affirmations to draw from when you just can't come up with any of your own.

Choose to be happy. As I've mentioned, happiness is 100% your choice. Everything you are doing and experiencing right now is a result of this and other choices that you have made throughout your life. In fact, when things are going wrong you can start to turn them around simply by acknowledging that on some level you have chosen this experience. Then, and only then, do you reclaim the power that you need to choose a different experience.

Choose to be optimistic. Things are never quite as bad as they look, especially if you keep working at staying positive. If you stay optimistic your creative mind will have all of the energy it needs to keep working. The end result of all that energy? You're likely to come up with a solution very quickly.

Envision your goals. Know your **why**! Keeping your 'eyes on the prize' will make setbacks and obstacles a lot less relevant to you. They're just small annoyances in your path, things that you have to walk around on your way to a much brighter future. The more you can connect today's activities with tomorrow's why the more motivated, excited and engaged you will be.

Smile more often. Smiling actually tricks your body's physiology. When you smile, your body and brain are flooded with happiness chemicals! You can also sit up straighter, stand up, move with purpose and with energy. Adopt the facial expressions and bodily movements of someone who knows where he or she is going, and of someone who has absolute certainty that they will get there, and believe me you will be on your way there.

Surround yourself with other happy people. I haven't mentioned this yet, but the support of other happy, successful people is critical. You always end up taking on the characteristics of the 5 people you spend the most time with. Do the people you are spending time with right now build you up, or do they bring you down? If they're bringing you down, look for other people to surround yourself with.

This is one reason why networking is so important—it's not *just* about helping people learn more about your business. It's also a great way for you to meet other happy, successful business owners. If they can succeed, you can too!

Have faith in yourself and the powers of the universe. The powers-that-be want you to be successful. If you keep your 'why' at the forefront of your mind and do everything you can do every single day then you *will* succeed.

Find upsides to adversity. Nobody *likes* adversity, but it almost always has something to teach us. If you can find that lesson you'll be able to leverage it to your advantage when the adversity has passed.

Finally, **learn to master your thoughts!** I can't stress enough how important this is. Negative thoughts will steal your energy, momentum and drive.

They will keep you and your business from becoming all that they can be. You may face many challenges in the days ahead; you do *not* need your mind to become your own worst enemy.

You need every part of your mind, body and spirit to be pulling for you, working as a coordinated team to give you what you need to succeed.

Business is supposed to be fun!

There is one final element of personal growth that I want you to master. I want you to be just a little bit less serious about your business. I'll wait for you to pick your jaw off the floor. I know that you've invested a lot of time and money into your business. I know that you have already taken some big risks; you have a lot riding on this. You've got a lot of dreams to pursue.

When so much is riding on your business it's very easy to succumb to your fears. Still, I firmly believe that business should be *fun*. You're following your passion and pursuing your dreams. You're doing something that most people only ever dream about doing and no amount of money could make the sacrifices and hard work of business worth it if it were all a labour of love.

Fun is one reason why I stress that you should be doing what you do best instead of trying to learn every skill in all areas of business. If you hate marketing, you're never going to have fun at it. If numbers confuse you then you're never going to have fun doing your own books and if you are a dedicated introvert then trying to be your own outside sales force will always be stressful for you, even if you learn every sales skill in the book.

You can apply the principle of fun in other ways as well. For example, one way to stop feeling stressed out about the results of your marketing is to make it a game.

Instead of waiting with baited breath to see if this or that marketing piece succeeds, you can just move on to the next one. You're making a game out of conducting a series of marketing experiments and you're waiting to see which experiments are going to pan out. The money that you make is nothing more than a score which you are racking up. When you start thinking of your business in those terms everything becomes a lot less serious. You can market your business and push your way to success while feeling a lot less anxiety. Instead of biting off your nails because you're not sure if you're going to get a good ROI on your direct mail campaign you can send it off thinking, "I wonder what my response percentage will be this time?

Can I beat the response rate I got last time?" If you don't, you'll simply go back and analyse why in an effort to get a better grasp on the rules of the game and how to use those rules to your advantage.

Finding the fun in your business keeps you adaptable, which is an important quality for any business owner. It helps you gently remove your ego from the equation so that you can do the right thing for your business. When you receive criticism you'll be able to adjust instead of taking it personally. You don't want your business to be your baby, your masterpiece, or the sum total of who you are because you're going to be a lot more prone to getting defensive about your every move.

If business is a *game* you are simply going to manoeuvre through it, playing it as well as you can to get the very best results that you can get.

I'm not trying to encourage you to be irresponsible about your business. Obviously I want you to play to win. I just want you to have fun while you're doing it. If your business stops being fun then I want you to take a step back and consider how you can inject your passion back into your work. Some businesses don't fail because the founder runs out of money. Some businesses fail because the founder gets burnt out, and doesn't want to do this any longer.

Getting support

The mind-set tips that I've been sharing will help you in every area of your business. But I'd like to take a moment to turn your attention back to marketing. After all, that's what this book is all about.

You have now had an opportunity to see the full extent of what it will take to successfully market your business. You now understand the role that marketing will play in the success of your business. There is one more thing that you must do in order to give your business its very best chance of success.

You need to be brutally honest with yourself. Get your marketing plan out and read it, page by page, line by line. Pay attention to your feelings as you do so.

While you can certainly use affirmations to turn those feelings around it's still a good idea to notice your initial reactions. If you feel stressed out, overwhelmed, or unhappy it's a good sign that you may not be the best person to handle your own marketing.

You could do all of the hard work of adjusting your attitude, and you could do all of the hard work of learning the technical skills you will need to execute your plan.

You could carve out the time to do this work. There's no question of that. The question is whether or not making the choice to do these things will tear you away from your primary love, and the business functions that bring you a sense of fun and fulfilment.

If you feel confident, happy, energised and secure, then you're in the right mental place to launch your own marketing plan. Some of the business owners who read this book will discover a hidden talent and drive to market their business. If all you feel is a sense of relief that you *finally know what to do* then I'm very happy for you. I didn't share all this information, thinking that nobody was going to use it personally. I want business owners to succeed, and I want them to do so at every stage of their business growth. If you can comfortably manage your own marketing at this stage of your business life cycle then I applaud you and I look forward to seeing the results you get.

There is of course, more to this than feelings. You also need to evaluate your own skills. Are you a good writer? Marketing requires a lot of writing work.

If you were the child who threw his or her pencil across the room when faced with a 500 word essay in school, you might be the wrong person to handle your marketing.

If you struggle to spell or use grammar correctly then you might be the wrong person to proof your own content. It may be that you can handle *portions* of your marketing but will be unable to take care of everything. You might choose to invest some portion of your budget into having professional videos made for your business, for example. It might be a good idea to send another portion of your business into a professional graphic designer or a web designer. This is a good solution for those who feel energised and enthusiastic about some portions of their plan but apprehensive and unhappy about other portions.

It may be that you don't have *all* of the skills to complete your plan, no matter how energised you may feel about it. If so, you may simply feel this energy as a result of getting your top-level thinking down on paper. You've already done the most important parts of it. It may be time to recognise that it's time to let someone else carry out the day-to-day work of that top-level thinking. After all, as you grow your company you will have employees whose job it will be to bring your vision into reality. There's nothing wrong with getting used to the sensation of creating a vision and then passing it on to others. After all that is what good leaders do.

If you're not the right person, then who is? You have several options: One option is to hire employees.

You may already have employees, of course, but most start-up businesses don't. I do not recommend hiring employees unless your current sales and your current growth can support the payroll. Marketing staff are usually the last staff members to be added to any in-house team. Your other two options are usually far more cost-effective.

Another option is to outsource. This is especially effective if you're going to handle some parts of your plan but don't have the skill or the time to handle other parts. There are legions of freelance writers, designers and other creatives who can help you launch your marketing efforts. Because you've taken the time to define your brand and create your plan you should find it relatively easy to instruct them on what to do and when to do it.

The third option is to hire an agency. This really does scare a lot of entrepreneurs, but remember: an agency might well be more affordable than you think. Certainly, the right agency is going to be poised to make you far more money than you're able to make on your own. A really *good* agency is an investment, not an expense. You just have to find that really good agency.

How do you do that? First, you can go looking for recommendations. If you're networking with other business owners this should be relatively easy.

You can just ask the most successful people in your group if they're using an agency, and, if so, which agency they are using. From there, you can go check out the agency's website.

Pay attention to your gut feelings as you do so, because each agency has a unique personality and outlook. If you don't feel comfortable with the way this agency is presenting itself or speaking to you on the web then you are not going to feel comfortable with the way the agency interacts with you in the future.

Next, you can go into the agency and start meeting some people. Some will want to give you a proposal right away. Avoid any agency who gives you a proposal with up-front fees. A £3,000 advance is likely to be well out of your price range anyway! If these sorts of numbers are the first ones you hear, keep looking. Many agencies will work with you on far more reasonable terms.

If the initial meeting goes well, you should ask to speak to some of the agency's other clients. Ask these clients to be candid with you about the results they have received. Are they getting more leads and more sales than they got before they engaged the agency's help?

If so, then you'll have a bit more information to help you calculate the potential return on investment that this agency could help you achieve.

Finally, you have to ask yourself whether or not you 'gel' with the people in this company. A good marketing agency *must* believe in you and your business in order to truly help you accomplish what you need to accomplish. They have to 'get' you, and you have to 'get' them. Here at WAM, for example, we don't work with anyone we wouldn't want to go down to the pub with.

That's not to say we do that all the time but we have to know we get on well and that we have absolute belief in the product or service the business is providing.

In the end, it will be up to you to choose your solution, just as you must choose your success. Will you pursue your 'why' with your whole heart and soul, or will you fall prey to the idea that you must do it all? Will you be in the 5% of businesses who succeed over the long haul, or will you be one of the 95% who fail in five years or less? It's all up to you.

No matter what you decide, it is unlikely that you will be able to achieve all that you wish to achieve on your own. I urge you to get all the support that you need to turn your business into a roaring success.

Purple!

#Quick Tip:

Do not listen to too many people, you will get conflicting advice and create confusion for yourself. When asking other people make sure they are qualified to give you advice.

The opinion of your best friend who is male and 30 isn't going to count for much, if your target market is female and 40+.

I believe in you! Now, believe in yourself, get out there, take massive action and live the dream so you can have the life you truly deserve!

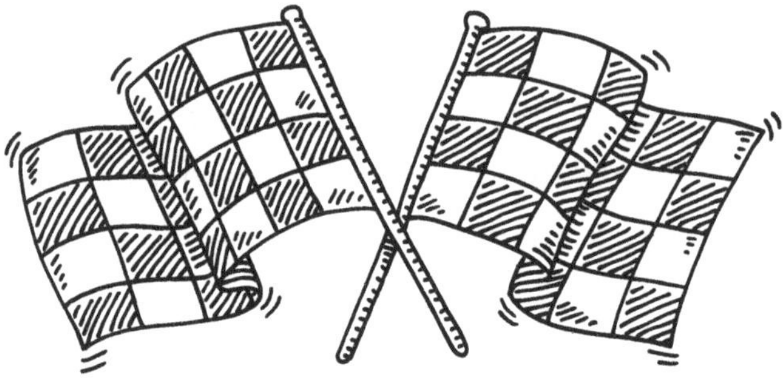

Lightning Source UK Ltd.
Milton Keynes UK
UKOW07f2250100215

246063UK00001B/33/P

9 780993 163005